Answer the Bell

Inventing Your Life as a Champion

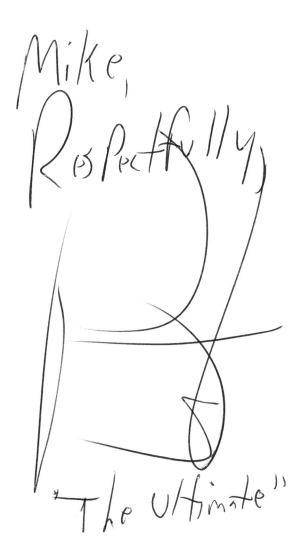

Mike,

Respectfully,

"The Ultimate"

Answer the Bell

Inventing Your Life as a Champion

Paul Vaden

Dandelion Books, LLC
www.dandelion-books.com

A Dandelion Books Publication
Dandelion Books, LLC
Mesa, Arizona

Library of Congress Cataloging-in-Publication Data

Vaden, Paul
Answer the Bell: Inventing Your Life as a Champion

Hard Copy Version
Library of Congress Catalog Card Number 2013933694
ISBN 978-0-9860145-8-1

Front cover art/concept/design by Anthony Cuomo
Back cover layout and book interior design by Accurance, www.accurance.com

All ATB book interview sessions were filmed and performed at Underground Elephant, Inc. headquarters.

Disclaimer and Reader Agreement

Printed in the United States of America
Dandelion Books, LLC
www.dandelionbooks-com

Contents

Dedication vii
Acknowledgments.. ix
Publisher's Note xiii

Chapter

  1. December 29, 1967 1
  2. Ali 3
  3. The 'Y' 11
  4. The Klondike..15
  5. Who Am I?..21
  6. Back To My Dream...27
  7. "Kid Ultimate"...33
  8. Wind Beneath My Wings 39
  9. Bowling For 160 47
10. Reality Check..53
11. "I Don't Bite!"..57
12. You're All I See..67
13. The Walk 73
14. Nemesis...83
15. Life Call: Weighing In 91
16. Answering The Bell 99
17. Paul Vaden Redux 111
18. The Hunger To Achieve..119

About Paul Vaden 131

For Dayne: "You are everything."

"Of all the titles I've earned in life, nothing gives me more pleasure than that of 'Dad'...being a real father to my son."

—Paul Vaden

Acknowledgements

No one can achieve these levels of accolades without infusions of emotional, spiritual, financial and positive support. I'm profoundly appreciative of the impact people have made on my life that inspires me to "Answer the Bell" (ATB) for myself and the world.

Thank you:

Carol Adler—for being a full breath of creative fresh air. Thanks for helping me get ATB to the finish line. I value your knowledge immensely and am honored to be a part of the Dandelion Books family.

Ma—for being the first person to love me and the last who'll ever give up on me. There's not a dollar amount that exists that can equate the love, spiritual guidance and support you've given me.

Dad—for giving me the foundation on right and wrong and how to treat others. For giving me the support to fulfill my dreams. I wish you were alive to witness these moments. However, there's not a day I don't think about or make a reference to you, to others. In everything I do I aim to carry the Vaden name to the highest honor. Love and miss you, Chief.

Danglo Vaden—for always telling me like it is no matter if the truth hurts, and for the loyalty.

Tanya Vaden—for being the sister I've always wanted—to love, protect and spoil. Stay in the fight, Tanya.

Lisa Vaden—for the greatest gift I will ever receive. Writing that note on the plane was one of my smartest decisions ever.

Steve "Lethal" Altman—round after round you're always there for me. I will never understand what I've done in this life to deserve your support. I thank God for your brutha'hood.

Kristin Farmer—for showing me what a gem truly is. Your mere presence is an inspiration; you beautify any atmosphere. I appreciate you beyond words.

Larry Dixon, Jr.—for knowing me better than anyone and yet still accepting me lol. Thanks for remaining a solid brutha' to me for four decades.

Uncle Ron Cheatham—for "the call" that changed my life. I miss you.

Kimberly Estell—12/21/1983—4Ever. IJCSLY & NCSGB.

Christopher Byrd—for being there for me during a time in my life when I needed a safe haven to restore from hurt, disappointment and betrayal. I don't know a person I laugh with more.

Howard G. Wright—for being more concerned when my last fight would be versus my next. You've always had my back and TRULY want nothing but the best for me.

Skipper Kelp—Skipper!!!! Words can't properly express your value to me. I'm blessed beyond measure to know and call you my little brutha. "This is Duck!"

Emmett Linton, Jr.—for elevating my game. "Snook," you instantly accepted me from the moment I arrived in Tacoma. I will never be able to thank you enough.

John V. Amodeo—for the effort you've brought to this ATB project. Thanks so much for your energy.

Jackie Robinson Family YMCA—for being my Disneyland and Motown all in one.

Robert Coons—for complementing my parental guidance and drilling in my head to never settle for getting hit.

Qualcomm, Inc.—for allowing me to integrate my talents on the land of innovation.

Underground Elephant, Inc.—for exemplifying the ideal company atmosphere and success I've longed to be a part of.

ACES, Inc.—for continuing to raise the bar and pioneer groundbreaking and fresh offerings. I'm proud to mesh talents with high quality leaders of excellence.

Tom Mustin—for taking my talents to whole new heights and helping me realize some great achievements. I'm forever grateful for the experience.

The Cheatham Family—for treating and supporting me like your own flesh and blood. We will always have Puyallup.

Bill "BDiddy" Davidson—for your friendship, time and expertise. For always pushing me toward positive situations.

Arnie "Tokyo" Rosenthal—for understanding my path and what makes me tick. I'm grateful for the endless conversations we've had beyond the scope of boxing.

Abel Sanchez—for giving me an educational odyssey of being a professional performer AND teaching me the uppercut!

David Love—for making boxing rehearsals and fight week so much fun! We worked extremely hard but had a blast doing it!

Dan Shea—for opening your wealth of knowledge and insights to me. I'm honored to be a part of the Donovan's team and call you my friend.

Mark Schlossberg—for your friendship and never leaving me ashore.

Bobby "G-Dub" Firtel—for being the first to take a chance on my early business and becoming such a loyal and trusted amigo.

Jerry McMahon—for exuding such class and your continued support.

Perry Falk—for bringing me into your family and for continued great times.

Jason Kulpa—for your undying support and friendship.

James Rayford—for your strength of belief in me and my talents.

Steve Farhood—for being the first writer to fulfill my vision by being featured in the magazine my dad use to purchase monthly for me as a child. Awesome journalist, even better friend!

Lauren Alexander—for your energy and infectious personality.

Joanne Conway—for your tireless work with the ATB brand. I'm indebted to you.

Jennifer Cota—for your energy and professionalism during the incubation stage of ATB.

In Memory:

Yvonne Polatchek (YSR)—for hearing me out and not letting me lose when I felt I was drowning in negativity. You were among the first to hear my book plans. I love you dearly and will see you again on the golden side.

Larry Dixon, Sr.—for always asking "what about Paul?" You involved me in so much with Larry, Jr. I experienced so many cool experiences because of you. I miss your phone calls.

Mo'Dear—for teaching me love and sensitivity. I miss your fried chicken wings, creamed potatoes and cornbread and viewing your excitement watching *The Price is Right.*

Grandma Geneva Coley—for taking me into your household on October 31, 1988 and giving me an opportunity to continue the dream.

Dr. Charles Miller—for providing me with the financial push so I could begin to Answer the Bell in 1988.

Byron Lindsay and Junior Robles—for helping pave the way.

Cliff Darden—for the intro to this fine art called boxing.

Ryan B. Cheatham—I miss you, "Little Man"…

Also:

The Jackie Robinson YMCA Original Boxing Team: Victor Worsham, Carl Blankenship, Drafton Bunch, Clayton Hill, Steve Hommel, Donald Wilson and Marcus Tucker. You all had an inspiring hand in fulfilling my lifelong dream.

San Diego Chapter for Juvenile Diabetes Research Foundation and "Rock the Cure"—until the referee halts this disease. I'm in the fight with you.

San Diego Chapter for Big Brothers-Big Sisters—for inspiring me to give and see life in the eyes of a child.

Thanks to Ernest Johnson Sr. and Old School Boxing Center— for your continued support and hospitality in allowing me to host my Boxing Seminars at your wonderful gym.

Publisher's Note

Recently, several of Paul Vaden's fans and colleagues who have experienced Paul's extraordinary "Answer the Bell" corporate presentations, seminars and inspirational talks, approached him and suggested he write a book.

"You always had role models who were champions," they pointed out, "because you were determined to find that secret formula of championship for yourself. Then, once you finally found it and became a world boxing champion, you used the same formula for becoming a champion in other aspects of your life as well.

"That still wasn't 'The Ultimate' Paul Vaden goal, however! You took your formula to the next level by developing your 'Answer the Bell' program. Through this program, you are now able to help others of all ages and from all walks of life become champions at their own life pursuits."

Rather than write a book solely from a first person perspective, Paul chose to incorporate parts of his life story written by others, and intersperse this narrative with his personal comments. At the conclusion of the book are several testimonials from his fans and colleagues.

It is a privilege and honor for Dandelion Books to "Answer the Bell" by bringing forth Paul Vaden's life work.

Carol Adler, President/CEO
Dandelion Books, LLC
www.dandelion-books.com

1
December 29, 1967

It was the late 1960s, a tumultuous time both in the United States and abroad. In 1963, President John F. Kennedy had been assassinated. In 1964, in the midst of marches, uprisings, sit-ins and sit-downs, the Civil Rights Act was passed. By 1965, the U.S. had sent troops to Vietnam and by late 1967 the war had already become a contentious football—especially after a call for deployment of still more troops to replace the unpredictable number of casualties arriving home in body bags.

In the final month of the year of 1967, the citizens of San Diego, home of Coronado Naval Base, millions of Americans took to the streets and demanded an end to a senseless war that was bleeding the country of its precious human and financial resources.

On December 29, 1967 in San Diego's Mercy Hospital, 18-year-old unmarried Gracie Mathis would not be thinking about assassinations, uprisings, far-off Asian conflicts, sit-ins, love-ins or other momentous events that might be shaking up the world anywhere else except here in the hospital, right now, inside her body.

Gracie was giving birth to a baby boy who would be given the name Paul Leon Hillard.

Childbirth is a transforming event for any woman and even more so for an unwed teenager. Yet Gracie was a strong woman who had the love and support of her parents and extended family. When she'd first learned of her pregnancy, Gracie declared, "I will have this child and give him or her all the love I can!" She had learned much from her parents and wanted to do what was right.

Paul never had a chance to meet his other parent, but Gracie was lucky. A year and a half after her baby was born, Gerald Vaden, a man with a big heart and love for children, came into her life. Gerald, who was a member of the staff at the same hospital where Paul had been born, was more than happy to serve as the baby's surrogate father.

"Gerald Vaden became my real father," says Paul. "A transplant from the Brownsville section of Brooklyn, this man who could neither read nor write, raised me to be the man I am today. He and my mom provided the structure I needed. They were always there for me. Our home was my refuge. It was a warm and loving environment.

"The house was typical of those in the area: one story, flat-roofed with a small front yard and an area for play. Many of the houses had grates on the windows and a fence; we had neither. And we had no garage, since we didn't own a car. The play area in the front was small, but for me, it was adequate. Since San Diego has warm, dry summers and mild winters, we spent a lot of time outdoors."

Even though Paul loved to be outside, another big draw was the television in the den. From the time he was four years old, he would be riveted to the screen watching events taking place in a large arena between two individuals who danced around a ring exhibiting clever hand and footwork while the crowds cheered and booed and sometimes went wild—and then, every so often, someone would *ring the bell*…

For this four year old, it was a circus and carnival all rolled into one huge grandstand performance. He was captivated.

2
Ali

"I want to be like him," boasted four-year-old Paul, pointing to Muhammad Ali whenever TV sportscasters mentioned his name or showed the great boxing champion in action.

Already by 1964, Ali had won the heavyweight championship and had ushered in what is known as the golden age of boxing. By the '70s, boxing had become a mega-million dollar box office extravaganza.

Mesmerized by the Ali "Shuffle" and unique fighting style, spectators went wild. Never in the world of boxing had anyone captivated the fans and delivered such an extraordinary display of athletic prowess.

Paul would stand in front of the TV transfixed, watching Ali's every move. "More than anything else, even at that young age, I wanted to be a world boxing champ like Ali. He was my hero. I told myself if he could do it, so could I!

"'Paul! Watch what you're doing!'

"I looked down at the tilted half-empty glass in my hand and at the milk on the floor. 'You've got to be more careful,' my mom scolded, smiling and shaking her head as she motioned for me to step aside so she could clean up the spill."

The Vadens lived in San Diego's poorest neighborhood amidst Mexicans, African Americans, poor whites and newer transplants from Viet Nam and Cambodia. Paul's idea of a good time was a birthday with homemade chitlins, black-eyed peas and yams. Those comfort foods were always a treat.

"The houses were so close together, we got to know all the neighbors. Right next door on my Street—'Z' Street—was Mr. Cliff Darden, a Navy vet who'd boxed when he was in the service."

By the time Paul was five he'd learned that Mr. Darden kept boxing gloves, posters, audio tapes of James Brown, and other boxing memorabilia in his garage.

"Mr. Darden's garage was magical. I liked the smell of the boxing gloves and then, putting them on…!! That was really special. They were smooth and felt good.

"I wondered, 'Could I do this? Could I learn how to box and become a champion like Ali?'

"Mr. Darden also had a microphone. On TV at the boxing events all the announcers used microphones… and then there was Michael Jackson and the way he used the mic… what a performer!"

Muhammad Ali and Michael Jackson were Paul's heroes.

"'I want to be a world boxing champion,' I announced to Mr. Darden.

"'You do, young man?'

"I noticed the smile on his face and the nod he gave me. 'Can you stand the punch?'"

Darden gave him "the eye" and waited for the boy's reply. "Can't waste my time on somethin' that's here today, gone tomorrow. Got to stick with it, son. Understand?'

"I straightened my shoulders. Now it was my turn to give Mr. Darden 'the eye.'

"'Yes, sir!' I declared.

"I knew Mr. Darden was thinking *the kid's got spunk, that's good. A good start.* 'But aren't you the one that's always falling over or bumpin' into somethin'?" Darden gazed at me intently.

"Yeah, you heard right. I do get into some messes and lose my balance. But I can learn, I want to learn and I'm ready." As I gazed up at him, I half-expected him to tell me to forget it and go play with the other kids.

"'I sure wanna try,' I repeated several times. 'There's one thing, though,' I added."

"What's that?" asked Darden, trying to hide his amusement at young Paul's earnestness.

4

"My mom can't know anything. She don't like boxing."

Darden laughed heartily. "Most don't 'til they see results. She'll come around, you'll see!"

The smile on young Paul's face sealed the deal. He knew he was home free.

"It will be our secret, provided it's not a problem," Darden reassured him.

Eventually Paul's father became aware of his frequent visits to Mr. Darden's garage. Since he and Darden were good friends, Gerald Vaden endorsed his son's passion, giving him the encouragement he needed.

Paul Vaden's boxing education had begun! Soon Darden garage visits became a ritual. Young Paul was in his element.

"I could tell Mr. Darden was impressed with my determination. Even though we were too poor for me to have a bicycle like some of the kids in the neighborhood, I didn't care. I had Cliff, the boxing gloves, the punching bag, James Brown's music and the mic. I felt like I was one lucky kid!"

Young Paul started to show promise. Soon the punches got faster and more on the mark.

"Although our family moved a couple of times, our new homes were in the same neighborhood in Southeast San Diego. It didn't matter. I could still walk to my magic garage. I was a happy kid with a dream."

Cliff Darden realized the young boxer had something else besides a natural talent for the gloves. It was that sterling quality that separated wannabee's from authentic achievers.

Whenever Paul delivers one of his "Answer the Bell" presentations, he reminds his audience that the source of all greatness, whether in the boxing arena, on stage, in the orchestra pit, or in the artist's or writer's studio, is a combination of guts, tenacity, ingenuity, flexibility and passion.

Already as a young boy Paul saw and felt these qualities in Muhammad Ali and other great champions. Ultimately they became the backbone of his practice sessions.

Paul was determined not to fail Cliff Darden or his family, and most of all, not to fail himself.

"I've trained a few boxers in my day," Darden reminisced to Paul's father in later years. "In young Paul, I saw the passion and the hunger so much needed in order to stick with it. I knew he had promise—oh yeah, I knew he had promise even at age five."

"Cliff Darden was my mentor, my coach and my friend," says Paul. "He became the first person who believed I had a future in the ring. I owe a lot to those smelly, dank venues, like Darden's garage. These were the places where it all started."

Soon Paul became familiar with all the earlier TV reruns of Muhammad Ali's famous fights.

Born Cassius Marcellus Clay, Jr., at age 22, immediately following his February 25, 1964 upset title win over Sonny Liston, cited by *Sports Illustrated* as the fourth greatest sports moment of the twentieth century, Clay changed his name to Muhammad Ali.

In 1967, Ali refused to obey the draft and enter the Army, costing him his boxing license for 3½ years. The three-year hiatus imposed by the boxing commission for Ali's refusal to be drafted for combat caused an uproar. Ali was quick to defend his decision not to serve with the retort: "No Vietcong ever called me a nigger!"

When Ali, nicknamed "The Greatest," regained his boxing license in 1970, he fought two comeback fights against Jerry Quarry and Oscar Bonavena in an attempt to regain the heavyweight championship from Joe Frazier. Paul loved to watch highlights of the Frazier fight, billed the "Fight of the Century."

"When I was six years old, on October 30, 1974, I have vivid memories of listening to Ali's world-famous 'Rumble in the Jungle' fight in Zaire, Africa, against undefeated world heavyweight champion George Foreman.

"The fight was only available on closed circuit, so we listened to it on radio. On the night of the match, my dad and Tim, a family friend, and I sat in the den in front of the radio waiting for the fight to begin.

"I was young, but I could feel the tension and the excitement. We all wanted Ali to win, yet we knew he was up against a fighter whose sheer size and punching power were legendary.

"My dad paced a bit and finally sat down, nervous like the rest of us… Mom came in with snacks and joined us… For Ali, so much depended on this match. Would he be able to recover his former world title from 'Big George' The Giant and prove to be 'The Greatest' after all?

"I was too young to know anything about boxing strategy, but I'd seen video clips of Foreman and I could visualize this hulking mass of muscle and brawn ready to tear into Ali. No wonder we were tense!

"I'll never forget the outcome, when we learned Ali had won. That small den in my folks' house shook from the jumping and hugging and screaming!"

Throughout his entire boxing career, Paul treasured that magical night. Whenever the going got tough or the odds seemed insurmountable, Paul would recall this memorable fight. "Ali was my inspiration, my role model."

If "The Greatest" could be a world champ, so could Paul Vaden!

"One day Mrs. Murchinson, Paul's third grade teacher at Horton Elementary School, asked the children what they would like to do one day when they grew up.

"Grinning broadly, without hesitation, I announced to her and the entire class, 'I'm going to be world boxing champion.'

"Some of the kids in the class giggled, but Mrs. Murchinson looked at me, raising her eyebrows and said, 'Well, Paul, that's quite a goal. Let's see what comes about.'

"That moment meant a lot to me," recalls Paul. The goal, the vision and the dream were already fixed in my mind. To state out loud that I wanted to be a world boxing champion meant that I took myself seriously."

In third grade Paul realized for the first time that his last name was registered "Hillard" and not "Vaden."

The matter may have been of little concern to Paul if he hadn't met his biological siblings who were attending the same school.

"Actually, a year later, in fourth grade, my biological brother, Marco, although a fifth grader, was in the same class, since it was a combined fourth and fifth grade class.

"But it was in third grade that it became an issue for me when one of the girls at school enjoyed talking a lot about my situation to anyone within earshot. She would tell them all about how I was her little brother.

"This was too much for me and far more than simply Mrs. Murchinson using my wrong last name. I had to find out what this was all about. How could those kids be related to me?

"I knew the only two people who could answer these questions were my parents, so as soon as I came home from school I asked them straight out to tell me where the name 'Hillard' came from.

"At the age of eight I was still too young to realize it could be a sensitive matter that my parents hadn't discussed with me yet because they wanted to wait until I was old enough to understand. Now, however, they had no choice.

"They explained to me that even though Gerald Vaden was not my biological father, he was my real father in every other way. They reassured me they planned to have my last name legally changed to 'Vaden.'

"My parents sent me to school with a permission slip to Mrs. Murchinson requesting that from now on I be called 'Paul Vaden.' Mrs. Murchinson complied, but still I had to deal with those Hillard kids! I did get the pleasure of having three or four good fights against Marco Hillard, who thought he could beat and bully me. BIG mistake!"

"By age eight I had become the oldest of three siblings, a brother named Danglo and a younger sister named Tanya.

"Every week Dad would come home with a special treat for each of us. Danglo and Tanya usually asked for candy but I had my own special request. In advance I'd tell my dad firmly: 'No treats for me this week. I'm saving up for the next issue of *The Ring. That* will be my treat!'

"My dad understood and complied, for more than one reason. Since he couldn't read himself, he was delighted that his eldest son was already literate and an avid reader of *The Ring* magazine, known as the bible of the boxing industry. He was also impressed that I was willing to sacrifice weekly treats in order to be able to afford a more costly one with a much higher value.

"I didn't mind sharing my bedroom with Danglo, especially since I was scared of the dark. When Danglo was there I felt much safer.

Danglo played with his toys but I had my boxing magazines. Every month I couldn't wait to devour the latest issue of *The Ring!*" In addition to great photos, *The Ring* carried all the latest information about every notable boxer, with ranking charts and detailed descriptions of each major event. For boxing aficionados, *The Ring* magazine was a must.

"Each of us had chores. As soon as I was old enough, I was responsible for washing the dishes and sweeping up around the house. Sometimes I'd be so engrossed in reading my boxing magazines, I'd fall behind in my chores and have to be reminded.

"I was a mama's boy—very respectful and conscientious—but I loved that magazine!"

What would it be like to step into the ring wearing a splendid robe, hands laced into those leather gloves, with thousands of spectators cheering him on?

3
The 'Y'

Perched on a hill overlooking the San Diego Freeway is the city's YMCA with a large mural visible to the thousands of motorists making their daily commute, of the man who broke the color barrier in baseball in 1947.

Jack Roosevelt "Jackie" Robinson (January 31, 1919 – October 24, 1972) was the first African American to play Major League Baseball in the modern era, ending racial segregation that for six decades had relegated black players to the Negro Leagues.

The YMCA was a fitting institution to pay tribute to Robinson. Since its founding in 1844, the 'Y' has been known as a place for young people to socialize, learn a number of valuable skills and receive mentoring from caring citizens and leaders of the community.

The Y has also served as a refuge for children living in difficult and often hostile urban and rural environments. Many who passed through the front door of the Y emerged several years later as young leaders ready to accept the challenge of creating a life devoted to excellence.

Mounted on the walls of the Jackie Robinson San Diego Y are glass cases displaying baseball, basketball and weight lifting trophies honoring past and present members' triumphs. Jackie Robinson would have been proud to have his name and reputation linked to the San Diego Y.

He would have been equally proud that a young, somewhat clumsy young man named Paul Vaden would consider the Y his second home, a place that would welcome and support his vision to become a world boxing champion—and a champion of life as well.

Like Muhammad Ali, Robinson became another great role model for Paul. Robinson was a trailblazer and trendsetter, a man who made his name in spite of a hostile climate.

"My story begins with Cliff Darden and continues at the age of eight with the Jackie Robinson YMCA."

"During the summer of 1976 when I was eight, my father and I visited the Jackie Robinson Y to sign up for summer camp. I didn't know what to expect besides baseball, basketball and a few trips.

"As soon as I learned there was a boxing area I wanted to see it. My dad and I headed toward the place where we were told it was located—and then I saw the ring!"

"Mr. Robert Coons was the Y's Program Director. We learned that he was the man we needed to see in order to sign me up for activities.

"I asked Mr. Coons if I was too young to box. He gave me a quick look-over and said, 'No, son, you can get involved. Are you sure you want to do this?'

"I looked up at my dad, silently pleading, 'You know I want in!' A $5.00 fee was required.

"My dad's response was firm. 'Son, I'm giving you a two-week trial. You hear? A two-week trial.'

"'Okay, okay—two weeks.' I was overjoyed. Two weeks. A lifetime! Mr. Coons was smiling broadly.

"And then I saw the poster on the wall of my hero, Muhammad Ali, clobbering George Foreman with a flush straight right hand in the famous 1974 Rumble in the Jungle bout.

"When I saw that picture of Ali, the deal was sealed. With my hero overlooking my every move, I knew I had to give it my all. Ali 'The Greatest' was looking at me and telling me I could do it—it was like he was talking to me. I knew I couldn't disappoint him!

"Although Robert Coons had a sports background in football—when he was in college he played on the team—his major interest was youth development. He was wonderful with kids, which is why he was a perfect candidate for administering the Jackie Robinson YMCA boxing program."

Fortunately, boxing mentors were also readily available. A group of high schoolers—Victor Worsham, Drafton Bunch, Carl Blankenship, Clayton "Gooney" Hill and Steve Hommel—had experience in the ring and enjoyed coaching upcoming boxers.

"My dad's two week warning wasn't in the cards—from the start I was in, and going at it 100%.

"Since I didn't have a bike, I would take the Number 4 bus to the Y every day. The fare in those days was 25 cents and it was an easy commute, just a ten-minute ride or a 15-minute jog for me.

"As soon as I arrived I'd go to the boxing area—I felt right at home. And always looking down at me was the picture of Ali, my idol."

Part of Paul's exercise routine was jumping rope and sprinting up the hill outside that overlooked the freeway. He also got into the ring suited up, with his boxing gloves laced on.

"Soon I was sparring with my cousin, Larry Dixon, Jr., and Eddie Richardson. They were both on the same level as I was. In fact, Larry went on to have a successful career as an amateur and professional welterweight. So, right from the start, I was in good company.

"I was nervous to spar. It was new—in fact, I hated sparring— but it was part of the program."

Paul put his heart and soul into his regimen. He listened to the coaches and did all the warm-up exercises before entering the ring. Once inside, he had his headgear, mouthpiece and gloves adjusted. He was eager to show off what he had learned.

The coaches were impressed with his hand speed and his agility. Paul was no longer a clumsy, awkward novice. Now he had command of himself and was starting to show serious promise.

School, homework, TV, movies and sports were the mainstays of Paul's growing years. With his fixation for boxing, it wasn't surprising that the 1976 film, *Rocky,* starring Sylvester Stallone, left a lasting impression. Portraying a small-time boxer earning money as a collector for a loan shark in Philadelphia's 'hood, Stallone gets his big chance when the world heavyweight champion, Apollo Creed, chooses Rocky at random as his opponent in a title fight.

To Mickey Goodmill, his gym trainer, Rocky is "nothing but a bum." Ironically, Mickey's sneering jibes goad Rocky on. It seems to be the perfect antidote he needs in order to prove to the world that he isn't just a mediocre boxer and ne'er do well. The fight with Creed is his big chance and he decides to give it his all.

Rocky loses the fight in a 15-round split decision, but wins the hearts of many with his heroic demonstration of guts and determination. For the first time in his life Rocky knows what it's like to feel good about himself.

"I loved the first Rocky film and the ones that followed. The first film, especially, was a real wake-up for me. I already knew, even at age eight, that I had to get my 'program' right."

During the same summer in 1976, Paul watched the telecast of Sugar Ray Leonard win the Olympic Gold Medal by defeating the great Cuban knockout artist, Andres Aldama.

It was a great triumph for Leonard. He was the talk of the boxing world.

"Sugar Ray became another great inspiration. By now I was already a part of the YMCA boxing program. I saw myself in the ring and being a champion!"

Before long, Paul was asked to participate in his first boxing match, an event that his mom, dad, sister, Tanya, and brother, Danglo, would attend.

The young boxer was ready to make his debut.

4
The Klondike

In 1976, eight-year-old Paul Vaden, with his family present, entered the ring at the Jackie Robinson Y for his first match. He wore standard Y attire: black trunks with red and green stripes, the familiar Afro-American colors, on the side.

Eventually he would have black and gold velvet trunks with "Sweet Paul" inscribed on the left front—an outfit made with a lot of love by Victor Worsham's mom. But that would come later.

"Those colors would stay with me throughout my career, as a tribute to Ms. Worsham after she passed away. But I also liked the colors."

The boxing event was sponsored by community donations. "It was the first time I learned about the importance of donations. If not for the donors, the event never would have taken place."

Years later, Paul would look back on this event with fond memories. "I never forgot my roots, the people who were there for me. Even when I made it to the top as world champion, I always remembered the Jackie Robinson Y. By the time I'd won the title, Toni Leonard—Sugar Ray's sister-in-law and a friend—put together several spectacular sequined robes. They all bore the same black and gold colors that I wore during most of my boxing tenure at the Y."

Matched up against a tough Todd Dozier, Paul performed well. But Dozier, who was two years older, was stronger. Those two years made all the difference. Also more experienced, Todd had the advantage of having already performed in front of a crowd.

"It was a standard three rounds, each round only one minute. I wanted to win one of the trophies the Y was giving to the winners. But, it was not to be.

"Even though I hit Todd often with hard punches and made his nose bleed, the outcome was not what I expected."

Todd won by decision after the three rounds. "I felt crushed. I remember asking, 'Where's my trophy?'

"I was told I did well, given the fact that Todd had been in the ring before and was older and stronger."

The initial setback only served to reinforce Paul's passion to get back into the ring and prove to himself that he could triumph.

In the next six fights that also included more fights against Todd, Paul beat Todd twice. In the third fight against Todd, Paul stopped him outright in the third round. This win restored Paul's confidence.

Once the school year started, Paul headed for the Y as soon as classes were over. By 4PM he would be in the gym warming up. "Even Coach Coons started to see the progress I was making. I thrived on his encouragement."

Soon Paul was ready for the first big trip outside San Diego in a series of exhibits called the "Chitlin Circuit."

"We had an old YMCA bus we called 'Betsy.' It got us to where we needed to go, rickety and old, yet it did the job. We drove to Grants, New Mexico for my first boxing exhibition in 1976. Mr. Coons and Mr. Dixon, my uncle, took turns at the wheel. We had some good times on that bus!"

Over the course of the next four years, the "Chitlin Circuit" molded young Paul Vaden into a solid boxer who started to gather trophies.

"I was becoming more self-confident. Beating Todd twice was the start. These wins also helped build my confidence for trying other sports."

Stronger on his feet and quick with his punches, Paul Vaden was becoming a focused, agile boxer.

"Actually, from my first trophy at Chicano Park to winning the National Junior Golden Gloves in Vallejo, California at age 10, I knew I was on my way.

During a photo shoot at Mercy Hospital, Gerald Vaden with Paul's gloves around his neck; and his sons, Paul and Danglo

**10-year-old Paul on heavybag for newspaper PR after winning the
National Junior Golden Gloves**

"It was on one of those 'Chitlin Circuit' tours in Mesa, Arizona, that Robert Coons saw me doing my homework. This was expected of me and everyone else—we had to keep up with our school work while on the road. But something caught Robert's attention. I was writing with my left hand.

"Why are you writing with your left hand?" I noticed the frown, a clear indication that something needed explaining."

Paul looked up at him. "Because ma says I'm left-handed. And I do write with my left hand."

Coons was apparently thinking, *he's done a lot of boxing as a right hander; Lord only knows how dangerous he'll become when I start teaching him to box southpaw!*

"Well, I'm going to show you how to switch," said Coons. "A switch hitter, just like with batters in baseball. When we return you will learn how to box southpaw."

"It was like learning all over again," says Paul. "I hated the initial process but I soon got comfortable with it. It just took awhile. In boxing as a right hander, I'd used my left jab more than anything else. But now as a southpaw, I had to use my right jab." What emerged was a real threat to his opponents: a multi-dimensional boxer who could box effectively from both stances while confusing his opponents.

Paul's former neighbor and first mentor, Cliff Darden, had introduced him to Carlos Bryant, a boxer from the navy. Bryant came to the Jackie Robinson YMCA to compete for the team.

"Cliff was amazed at the progress I'd made. I guess he saw in me a bit of himself and was proud that he'd played a major role in giving me my start. Cliff continued to serve as a mentor.

"The boxing team at the Jackie Robinson Y was only a year old when I started going there in 1976. When Coach Coons recognized my potential, immediately he knew I needed to have additional boxing exposure, so when I was only nine years old he arranged for me to start attending the Western Regional Golden Gloves events in Las Vegas with the older members of our team. At these events, aspiring boxers 16 years and older have a chance to perform and qualify for the National Golden Gloves.

"Just as Coach Coons predicted, the experience was invaluable, since most of our own team was in the Novice Division. I was able to watch, learn and talk with more advanced members and coaches of the other western U.S. boxing teams.

"These events greatly enriched my boxing education. In fact, this is where at age nine, I first met Tom Mustin. He was the coach of the Tacoma Boxing Team that had a score of Olympians and national champions. I would ask Mustin and his team all kinds of questions and mimic their boxing moves.

"All the boxers and coaches in the Western region, which included the Pacific Northwest, Arizona, Nevada and California, seemed to enjoy talking with me.

"At age 12 I'd become so advanced, even though I wasn't old enough to qualify as a participant, they invited me to be part of the Western Regional Golden Gloves first night as a 'Special Attraction.'

"For the first three years of the Western Golden Gloves events I had to stay at the YWCA, but when I turned 12, in addition to participating, I got to stay with the rest of the boxers and coaches at the Klondike Motel."

For a 12 year old, both of these concessions were monumental. Its gigantic sign alongside the barn-red motel's two-story structure was a famous landmark to travelers entering Vegas via the expressway, and with its $1.49 all-day spaghetti special, it was a popular tourist spot.

"Even when I ended up staying at the penthouse hotels in Vegas, a smile would come over my face when I thought of the kid who'd finally made it into the Klondike!"

As Paul continued to practice and learn from other boxers and coaches, he started to be recognized for his abilities as well as another special quality. The young boy's determination and drive told everyone this boxer had a mission and he wasn't going to let anything stand in his way.

5
Who Am I?

"I never knew we were poor until I went to Harvey A. Lewis Junior High School. No Disneyland for me. No Knott's Berry Farm. Oh, we would go to Balboa Park and the zoo, but I generally spent all my time at the Y. It was at Lewis that I really started to see a different world."

The school closest to his home was Samuel Gompers Junior High School, but his parents insisted on busing him to Lewis JHS. Later, Paul understood why.

"Lewis was predominately white. I didn't want to be bused to Lewis. I preferred to go to Gompers and continue my education in my neighborhood where I was comfortable. I now realize, however, that my parents were looking out for me. If busing was available for their children, they knew they needed to take advantage of it.

"At first I felt like a foreigner. Besides being one of the few black students, all I had to do was look at the clothes and the jewelry that some of the students wore to get the message."

It was exactly the type of social experience that Paul needed. By the time he was ready to go to high school, he no longer felt like a misfit.

After junior high, Paul started his sophomore year at Patrick Henry High School,

A large sprawling contemporary campus that opened in 1968, Patrick Henry was a considerable distance from Paul's neighborhood. As he boarded the bus each morning, he realized he'd become a member of one of San Diego's larger high schools that reflected the ethnic mix of a growing city. With over 2,500 students and a 57-acre campus, it was a big change from the small neighborhood schools that Paul had attended.

"I was just 14 when I competed and won the California Junior Olympic Regionals." At 100 lbs., by winning, Paul qualified for the 1982 National Junior Olympics in Colorado Springs.

When he first arrived in Colorado Springs, however, there was a problem. His given name on his birth certificate read "Paul Hillard." His name still had not been legally changed.

For Paul it was an upsetting reminder. He was Paul Vaden in every sense, and yet the official documents still listed his given name as Hillard.

"I wasn't sure which was harder—being called Paul Hillard, a name I didn't identify with, or the strict diet of eating just one tangerine a day to maintain my 100-pound qualifying entry!"

Paul was announced to the assembled crowd as Paul Hillard and it bothered him. He knew he had to have his parents make the necessary provisions to legally change his name.

In the semifinals Paul lost a split decision to the eventual five-time professional world boxing champion, the late Johnny Tapia. It would also be the last time when he would be introduced as Paul Hillard. This was a major relief for him.

Like a true champ, Paul was already preparing for the next event. "I needed to get my weight down to qualify for the upcoming National Junior Olympics in 1983 at St. Paul, Minnesota."

The outcome of the St. Paul event was not what Paul had expected. On the first night, he lost to the eventual national champion.

Suddenly, he started to question his ability. Were all the training, preparation and anxiety worth it?

He wasn't a quitter. He remembered what his parents, trainers, pastor and friends had said about life, its ups and downs and what it took to keep on keeping on… *Was it time to take a pass and move on to something else?*

Never!

And yet… and yet… An identity crisis ensued.

Added to his dilemma was his parents' announcement that they were splitting up.

Children of divorced parents go through changes. Some choose sides, others find solace in their studies or sports, and still others rebel, getting into drugs and hanging out.

Inside Paul felt like a wounded tiger. *What to do, what to do?* Should he continue on the same path? Did he have what it took to succeed, or should he just forget about the dream and pretend he was like everyone else—no one special, no one with big dreams?

He came to a compromise. He wouldn't give in and become ordinary. That wasn't possible because it wasn't who Paul Vaden was.

Instead, he decided to become someone who would be just as unique as a boxing champion.

Away went all the fond memories of the neighborhood garage, the gloves, punching bag, James Brown music and the mic... out went memories of Mrs. Murchinson and the third grade speech... away went the Jackie Robinson Y and the glory of the ring... hours of sparring followed by trophies and wins... "Chitlin Circuit," trips to Vegas, Junior Olympics... all of it was pushed to the furthermost recesses of his mind. *There! Gone for good... (or at least for now).*

It was 1983 and Michael Jackson's *Thriller* album was the Number 1 hit. The singer, complete with his red jacket, sequined glove and jheri curl created a fashion statement that captured young Vaden's imagination. The music as well as the lifestyle exemplified Coming of Age. It was a perfect escape for the young Patrick Henry High School teenager who was hurting bad inside. Very bad.

Before long he started to show up at school wearing the Michael Jackson Look, the superstar's familiar trademarked attire. Heads turned. The girls noticed and smiled.

It was his moment. "I got the jheri curl, black fedora, sequined glove and red jacket and became my own version of Jackson."

Friends at school started to call him Michael and he liked the attention. Walking down the halls of Patrick Henry, he would get high fives from the students and looks from the teachers. Some good, some not so good.

"It didn't matter. This was my way to express myself. My threads were mine, yet they allowed me to be someone else. I continued to be Michael Jackson in my mind. This went on for most of my high school years, right up to the 12th grade in 1986. I felt no pressure, now that I wasn't boxing.

"Basketball had always been my second favorite sport. In sixth grade I played basketball at the Y and led the league in scoring. During halftime of an NBA game at the San Diego Sports Arena I played in an All-Stars game, so it was a natural progression for me to continue playing basketball once I got to high school. I knew I could make the team. I was quick on my feet and after years of intense boxing practice, I also had enduring stamina.

"I tried out and made junior varsity, and then later, the varsity team. My teammates and I got along well. Soon I excelled and became captain of the team.

"Before that time, The Washington Bullets were my favorite team, but now I switched allegiances to the Lakers. This was in large part due to Magic Johnson. The major attraction besides his skill on the court was his personality.

"Also, the fact that Stu Lantz was on the faculty further cemented my commitment to basketball." Lantz, a former NBA basketball player, later distinguished himself as a sportscaster for the Los Angeles Lakers. "I was in his office on occasion not for reprimands, but to chat with him. During the entire time I attended Patrick Henry High School, I never disclosed to Stu anything regarding my boxing background."

Paul also liked the arts, theater and of course, music. With his alter ego Michael Jackson persona, he chose the classes that were less demanding.

"The most interesting thing that frightened me most was being forced to give oral presentations in front of the class. Oral projects that demanded a defense would be difficult. But it hardened me and made me more confident.

"My cousin, Larry Dixon, Jr., was my constant friend. He was with me from elementary school right through high school.

"Other than Larry, no one knew of my boxing background. In elementary school I used to try to pick on him in the schoolyard and I remember being flipped onto the ground and put in my place! Larry also started boxing just one week after I began at the Jackie Robinson YMCA.

"It's an interesting fact that when asked who has my number in boxing, I always state 'Larry Dixon, Jr.' Not only did he flip me on the playground, but he also got to know my every boxing move. He knows me probably better than anyone else."

"This was a traumatic time for me. At home, Mom maintained a normal day-to-day regimen that kept us united. I know deep down it was hard for her but she never showed it.

"At school I concentrated on being Michael Jackson and playing basketball. I never wanted any of my friends at school to know about the boxing and about my days at the Y. I'd lost my confidence in a boxing career. I could have impressed the girls and told them I'd won a lot of boxing matches and gone to the nationals, but I decided it was best to put all that aside."

It wasn't in Paul's DNA to boast, and given the shock of the Junior Olympic Nationals defeat in St. Paul, Minnesota coupled with his parents' breakup, right now it seemed best to leave it alone.

He did have a huge crush on a pretty girl who attended La Jolla High School. All he told her about himself was that he was a good basketball player and a popular guy with a lot of different friends. It was easier not to make waves or create problems for himself.

Predictably, with his abandonment of boxing, Paul's high school years were uneventful. His Michael Jackson "cover-up" had been a good ruse but deep down he knew it was just a temporary disguise, a distraction that had served its purpose.

It was time to make some changes, yet he needed funds to assist his mom and his brother and sister. He wasn't ready for the ring, at least not yet.

After graduation from Patrick Henry, 19-year-old Paul started working as a paint specialist at Montgomery Ward. "It was a start to keep a few dollars and help mom out." He had a job, a little money— life wasn't bad, yet it wasn't great, either. The dream of the young four year old still haunted him. He couldn't shake it off.

His mind drifted back to that musty garage just a few steps away from his home where it had all begun. The smell of the gloves, the feel of the leather, and the action—oh the action of the ring…

"During the summer of 1987, I got a phone call. It was a call that would change my life."

6
Back To My Dream

"Do you want to go to the Olympics?" It was Ron Cheatham, the Executive Director of Puyallup Valley Family YMCA in Washington State. I'd met Ron in 1983 when he was Executive Director of the Jackie Robinson Y and coincidentally, when he called I happened to be at the Y.

"It's time you got your priorities right and started thinking of boxing again," said Ron.

The Olympics! Who would turn down such a challenge?

"I didn't have to think twice! Ron spoke to me for some time, telling me that he wanted me to move to Tacoma, Washington and compete under the head coach, Tom Mustin."

All it took was an encouraging call from someone who knew he had a special talent. The charade he was going through being someone else and not focusing on his talents was about to end. The job at Montgomery Ward would go to some deserving young man or woman. He had to move on.

"I wasn't a quitter and I knew if others had faith in me, I damn well had to show myself I was up to it."

Paul was reluctant to tell his parents of the offer. "I really never left boxing. But I didn't want my folks to know what I was up to until I got my bearings and became re-acclimated again."

Paul started training hard. That summer of 1987, he began his regimen at Mission Beach, just north of his native city. His workouts at Hamel's Sports Center took place upstairs, away from suspecting eyes. Dan Hamel and his brother, Ray, owned the bike and sportswear spot on the boardwalk overlooking the scenic bluffs of the Pacific.

"The small boxing gym, complete with a few heavy bags, was a perfect spot for me. I asked Victor Worsham from my early Jackie Robinson YMCA days, to oversee the workouts. I wanted his assessment as I progressed. I made it clear to him that no one was to know. I wanted it to be highly secretive. You have to remember that it was a long four years since I'd taken this endeavor seriously. The beach nearby was an added incentive, since it allowed me to get my running done."

With the ocean breeze at his back and once again feeling the joy of doing what he loved most, Paul started regaining his confidence.

"Slowly but surely, my skills started becoming respectable again. My hand speed never left me. I did need to get my timing of hand and foot back. Boxing is all about speed. It can be a split-second affair."

Paul started to make progress and Victor noticed the improvement.

"I was ready to 'Answer the Bell.' Yet in order to get up to Tacoma, I would need some cash, and money was still hard to come by."

On a February morning, his dream became reality with the purchase of a plane ticket to Tacoma.

"Dr. Charles Miller, a friend of my dad's at Mercy where they both worked, was a boxing fan—a big fan. He respected my dad and had eventually gotten to know me. He insisted on paying for my airline ticket.

"I didn't tell anyone why I was going to Tacoma. Even Dr. Miller didn't know!

"On February 7, 1988, I went to the airport accompanied by my dad, Victor Worsham, Drafton Bunch and Carl Blankenship. All of these men were part of my life and represented my young YMCA days. They had been there for me in times of need. Today was no exception.

"As I got ready to say goodbye, my dad presented me with a ring to keep as a token of family strength. Victor, smiling broadly, started to clap and the others joined in." Paul knew the ring would not only be a special bonding with his family but also a symbol of the people who had worked hard with him to help him get this far. He wouldn't let them down. He touched the ring, knowing it would be his connection to home. It would also be a constant reminder of the faith they had in him. "I was representing them. I would never forget that!"

"As soon as I arrived in Tacoma, I immediately started training. It was like I'd never left! Sure, I had to regroup and reevaluate, but the gifts were there. Before long, I was sparring in the ring and eager to make the U.S. team."

Paul didn't disappoint the coaches, Tom Mustin and Lloyd Peterson. "At the Tacoma Golden Gloves, I beat a boxer named Frank Vassar. Vassar was a nationally ranked welterweight. I got to showcase my skills." Scouts, other trainers and the audience saw the raw talent.

"I was competing at 147 lbs. in the welterweight class. I was ready to prove to myself and anyone else that I was now in the game."

During the same year, Paul won the bronze medal at the U.S. Amateur Boxing Championships. Coming from obscurity to third place in a major event with less than two months' training under his new coach, Tom Mustin, reaffirmed not only faith in himself and his skills but also validated what the coaches knew all along—that he had what it took to go all the way to the top.

"The second match of the 1988 U.S. Championships in Colorado Springs was memorable. My opponent was from the Marines All Service Team who had no idea who I was or what I looked like.

"When Tom Mustin and I reported to the table to receive our boxing gloves, what the Marine saw was a tall scrawny guy with a Michael Jackson jheri curl and a big ingratiating smile.

"Without a moment's hesitation, he turned to his teammate, a smirk spreading over his face and gave him a high five in front of me, just to make sure 'the dork/douchebag/wimp' understood what was in store for him.

"Normally, boxers warm up by hitting boxing mitts with their coaches to get loose, but also show off their skills to get a psychological edge. This time I told Tom I wasn't going to hit the mitts to preview my gifts in front of this Marine. Oh no... not this time.

It was going to be way too much fun to watch this guy who'd pre-judged me by my appearance, smile and physique, to get the shock of his lifetime.

"From the moment the first bell rang until the final bell this man was in hostile hell and couldn't land a single blow on me while I delivered volumes on him. When it was finally over, the smirk had been replaced by an expression of relief as he congratulated me. I moved into the quarterfinals, jheri curl, big smile, skinny physique and all!"

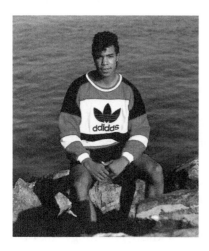

Paul, 20 years old, "finding his way back to his dream and a sea of possibilities"

Although Paul was now in the welterweight class, he lost in a split decision to qualify for the Olympic Trials. At the time he didn't consider it a major setback, since he realized he had two more chances to qualify in the future. By now, like a character in a Hollywood script, he knew he was the real deal—the Comeback Kid who was proving to himself and others that he wouldn't allow occasional challenges to overwhelm him.

"I went on in that same year to win the Western Regional Golden Gloves in Las Vegas. This was especially exciting, since they are the same Western Regional Golden Gloves events that I used to attend from the time I was nine years old—where I'd first met Tom Mustin, and where I was also a "Special Attraction" at age 12. And now I was competing for Tom's team, the one I'd held in such high regard as a child! I won both matches and qualified for the National Golden Gloves."

But as fate would have it, as it drew closer to the date of the event, Paul contracted a bad cold. "I kept asking myself: 'This isn't an ordinary cold. Is it the flu?'

"The combination of fighting a virus and dealing with a strict training diet of eating and drinking only once a day—a training diet I'd maintained since I was 10 years old—was too much for my immune system." At the National Golden Gloves in Omaha, Nebraska when Paul entered the ring, he was lethargic and ineffective.

It was a difficult loss for him and this time he took it personally.

"All the training and dieting, all the preparation... and now, feeling sick and going into the ring and losing..." The disappointment was overwhelming. He did *not* want to be a loser. *He was not a loser!*

"I knew I had to come to terms with myself. The loss gave me an opportunity to reassess my situation. I used it as an example of what not to do. I'd look at the video and realize, yes, the cold and being sick were important parts of it, but I had to put more emphasis on my talents.

"I started to work out even harder, sparring more and watching every intake of calories into my body. I made the Omaha event into a positive learning experience."

In June of 1988, Paul participated in several important boxing matches. "The Western Olympic Trials were being held in Houston, Texas. I qualified to box and I was ready for it. I beat five contenders, including Ernie Chavez and Raul Marquez—all five fights by unanimous decision verdicts.

"I defeated Marquez in the semi-finals. Marquez would go on to be the fighter who would follow me as a professional world junior middleweight champion."

In the finals of the Western Olympic Trials, Paul also defeated Booker Kidd of Dallas by unanimous decision.

What a change from Omaha!

At 147 lbs., Paul Vaden qualified for the Olympic Trials, which he accomplished in less than five months of training. Yet he would still have to box others in order to make it to the Olympics.

The finals were held in Concord, California. He would end up fighting world amateur champion Kenny Gould which resulted in a split decision. The officials gave it to Gould.

"I was in the locker area when Mr. Gould, Kenny's dad, approached me. He looked me straight in the eye and said, 'You won that fight. You beat my son and I just wanted you to know.' He said this right in front of his son!"

31

Paul was deeply touched by Mr. Gould's candor. His confidence restored, he was ready for the next venture thrown at him by his coaches.

"I looked at the ring that Dad gave me and felt myself smiling. Despite being divorced from my mother, the ring drew me closer to the person who never gave up on me." Paul decided not to be bitter, but to look to the future. He would continue to improve his skills.

"I flew back to San Diego feeling disappointed but more determined than ever to prove to everyone that I had only just begun to make my mark."

Like most people on their way, he reflected on the past year and realized he had performed far beyond his wildest dreams. The next year would be his big chance.

"Coming back from the disappointment at Concord, I began to dream even bigger. My life and focus level would never be the same. I started to work out with even more intensity. Soon I was 156 lbs. and now competing in the light middleweight class."

Paul returned to Tacoma where he trained for the next several months. As he gained more confidence, his trainers confirmed that he was ready to take his talents to the next level.

Paul also started to challenge himself with a list of objectives for transforming his status from amateur to world class athlete.

Paul's "To Do List" became his bible. He referred to it, relied on it, learned from it and improved on it. Like a religious zealot, he made his mantra "Never relent." It kept him going. He reviewed the list constantly and took it with him everywhere.

"I was no longer the young kid hiding behind the Michael Jackson sequined glove. I decided I needed a new identity. I became 'Kid Ultimate.'"

He liked the idea of having a name attached to his goal. Many boxers have branded themselves with a name: "The Greatest," "The Truth," "Iron Mike," "The Manassas Mauler." Paul Vaden would become "Kid Ultimate."

"Kid Ultimate"—the sound of it appealed to him. He wouldn't fail. He couldn't. It wasn't just a ring, a bout, or an arena anymore. The ring was his stage. Now he was ready to make his mark as a performer, soon to be noticed and acclaimed.

7

'Kid Ultimate'

In 1989, as a participant in the World Games, "Kid Ultimate" traveled to Moscow.

"First we stopped in Amsterdam. I saw a different culture and a city that was much more open than any place in the U.S. I was like a kid!" The Dutch capital was indeed an education for the young American on his first trip abroad.

Paul and his group were given a complete tour of the colorful city. In the notorious Red Light District they saw women plying their trade openly, with government approval. The cubicles aligning the district, their own private domain, welcomed the curious from every part of the world.

"Quite a sight to see. Legal and controlled by the state, the women were taken care of and no one seemed to give it a second thought. Most of them were just sitting there, doing nothing. Occasionally, they'd look up as we walked by. A smile, a casual wink. Then back to filing their nails or brushing their hair. I kind of felt sorry for them, wondering what lured them to this life."

On their boat tour Paul and his group saw centuries-old build-ings—"pointy, scale-like structures, narrow and close together or attached, lining the cobblestone streets. The houses had brackets on the outside to move furnishings up to the second and third levels or beyond. So unique!"

He enjoyed the house boats with their Holland tulips and other blooms, another major tourist attraction. They also visited the Rijksmseum that housed the works of many great Dutch painters, including Van Meer, Bosch and Van Gogh. Also on their tour was the Anne Frank Museum, a tribute to the young Jewish victim of the Holocaust.

As the boat meandered along the canals, Paul was aware of the juxtaposition of old and new: step-like buildings where the Dutch masters had lived and painted, mixed with motorcycle gangs and tattooed young people smoking pot as luxury vehicles sped by...

"Our next stop before Moscow was West Germany, where our training sessions would begin."

As soon as they arrived in Germany, Paul and the other participants launched into a rigorous schedule that included sparring, jumping rope, jogging, and keeping a strict diet. Then, on to Russia.

The Rossiya Hotel was adjacent to Red Square, with a clear view of Lenin's Tomb, the Kremlin and St. Basil's Cathedral.

"Before the match, we visited Lenin's tomb. Since we were a select group, we were able to jump ahead of the lines of spectators."

As they entered the mausoleum that was a memorial to the revolutionary Communist hero, Paul and the others realized they were witnessing history in the making. Perestroika and glasnost would ultimately rule the day; the once formidable Soviet system was about to collapse.

Crowds in the square were large but peaceful. It was indeed a historic time. Yet for Paul, it was another arena that held his full attention. The World Amateur Championships would give him an opportunity to excel and get noticed. Participation in the world games would be a good stepping stone.

Following the 1989 season, Paul was selected as a First Team All-American. It would be an important year in which he would be ranked Number One in the nation at 156 lbs. He would also become a U.S. Olympic Festival Gold Medalist and win scores of other honors.

On January 10, 1990, a team dual event, The USA vs. the then Republic of Yugoslavia, took place at Rapid City, South Dakota.

"On January 8th, my teammate and treasured 'brother' for life, Skipper Kelp, cut my Michael Jackson jheri curl, at my insistence. I was coming into my own!

"I beat my Yugoslav opponent, then returned to San Diego for a few days before resuming my training in Colorado Springs."

People were starting to take notice. Trainers, sportswriters and the public as well were getting to know Paul. He'd finally started to get some much needed press. The local Tacoma newspapers wrote several favorable articles about the young upstart from San Diego. Yet his hometown media did little or nothing to cite his accomplishments.

"I was getting press coverage in Washington State and other areas throughout the world, but very little action from my local press. Go figure!"

In addition to the Gold Medal at the U.S. Championships, he would triumph by stopping the Canadian champ in the third round, repeating as a First Team All-American and ranking light middle-weight. Paul would close his amateur career with a bronze medal at the Goodwill Games held in Seattle.

My mother, Gracie Vaden, holding my plaque after I was honored as Amateur Star of the Month for February, March and April, 1990

Paul continued to hone his skills, practicing daily at the Olympic Training Center in Colorado Springs. Workouts were long and intense. "After the European trip, I realized it was a big world and I wanted to be part of it. I liked the attention from the trainers and the smiles from the ladies too!"

"Kid Ultimate" was now intent on turning professional. At 23, Paul was in his prime. His unique style coupled with his quick hand and foot movements got the attention of major players within the boxing establishment.

"In 1989 while I was still a member of the U.S. team, the late Ernie Wright, Sr., former NFL football player and agent, became my advisor. Mr. Wright was a longtime family friend. His youngest child, Howard, has remained one of my best friends. We had silently agreed that I'd turn pro following the Goodwill Games.

"My pro career got launched with my own syndicate, Ultimate Sports Associates. It was comprised of five businessmen. I had every major promoter wanting to align me with their promotional stable. One of the individuals who came on board was Dr. Nolan Johnson. I'd known Dr. Johnson since I was nine. He volunteered his time as ringside doctor of many of my amateur matches that took place at the Jackie Robinson Y.

"Another member of the syndicate was Bob Fox, former Vice President of Marketing for Coors. In 1992 Bob would become my sole manager.

"The goal was to allow me to chart my own course before having to deal with the Don Kings and Bob Arums of the world."

Paul's first professional fight took place in 1991 in Albuquerque, New Mexico. The young San Diego kid now known as "The Ultimate," was ready for prime time. "I even had my own 'The Ultimate' line of apparel!"

Paul won his first match. "My second fight was in Tijuana, Mexico and I won by decision. This was immediately followed by my next fight in Del Mar, California. There was coverage—TV, newspaper, lots of family and friends. I won in the second round—a knockout-punch that left my opponent dazed on the canvas." The crowd loved it.

Within that same year, 1991, Paul won three more fights: the first by decision in Tijuana; the second, a knockout fight outdoors in the first round before an admiring crowd at Lakeside, California; and the third, another win by decision, at the LA Forum.

Paul Vaden was starting to get a following. The press, trainers and spectators saw something special. It was all good, until the night of the match in Tijuana, a border city so close to his home.

The loud, boisterous crowd consisted of many local Mexicans eager to support their own. "My mom was in the audience. I heard a lot of screaming and shouting and thought nothing of it. I was there to fight and get a win."

Paul did his job: a TKO complete with a broken nose—and this, to the favorite of the crowd!

All hell broke loose.

With the victory came mayhem: too much booze, too much anger and not enough security. "I was really concerned for my mom. I had to be escorted by my trainer and a makeshift entourage to the dressing room. I kept asking about my mother. The crowd was throwing bottles, there was broken glass everywhere and people were getting hurt... they were ripping up programs and newspapers... I was grateful to hear that my mom was surrounded by the NFL players who had come to support me."

This experience was an important lesson for Paul. He realized he needed to make sure every venue ensured safety for his family and fans.

Even though the victory was bittersweet, it was a good fight. "I knew my left was stronger than my right, due to my being a converted southpaw." Coupled with his quick hands, Paul always had the advantage of speed—he could perform the "dance of the ring" at his opponent's peril. Watching him box was both a fight and a performance.

"I wanted to emulate Sugar Ray Leonard and of course, Ali, with their quick dance-like steps."

"Boxing became theater for me. My concert was my fight in the ring. I was in charge!"

As he approached his twenty-fourth year in 1992, Paul Vaden was part of the undercard on a nationally televised ABC boxing event. "My idol, Muhammad Ali was in the audience. Terry Norris was the main event. It was held at the San Diego Sports Arena, so I had a good hometown crowd. My new attire was part Michael Jackson, complete with a robe with epaulettes. I fought a good fighter named Richard Evans, originally from Philadelphia, and a stable mate of Terry Norris. I won by decision."

On April 29, Paul fought another match, again at the San Diego Sports Arena, and won against Fred Thomas.

"I remember after the fight my mom scolding me, telling me as she looked me directly in the eye: 'Stop playing around in the ring! You're a fighter, not a dancer!" My dad came to my defense, adding: 'He's playing his opponent and strategizing him. Give him some slack. He knows what he's doing.'

"My parents were divorced, yet both were very supportive of me. Dad was living nearby, at the home of Mr. and Mrs. Payton Williams, the couple who had raised him since his arrival at age 16 from Brooklyn."

Paul's reputation was growing. "I saw myself as an artist as well as a performer. I tried to perfect my craft so the crowd would come away knowing they'd experienced something different… that the fight would be one they would talk about over a beer or at the dinner table.

"I wanted to be in complete control of the ring. I wanted to strut my stuff, show off my skills, and take the wind and sails out of my opponents. What could stop me?!"

Yet something did. Fate stepped in and demanded his attention. It came on a Sunday morning while his mom was at church services and his sister, Tanya, was at home alone.

8
Wind Beneath My Wings

Tanya Vaden heard a knock on the door. Then another knock. "Let me in!" shouted a man's voice.

The knocking grew more insistent, followed by more shouting.

Tanya was terrified. Whoever it was sounded like he was drunk. Recently there'd been some robberies in the area.

It would be so easy for someone to break in… Tanya dialed her brother Paul, who had become the man of the family since their parents' divorce.

"I had just come back from six miles of jogging. I was training hard at the time, since I had a fight only three days away. 'Hey Tanya, what's going on?'"

"Paul, someone's knocking at the door, a man. He sounds like he's drunk!"

"At once I was alerted. Although I tried not to be over-protective of my younger sister, I didn't like the sound of her voice. 'Don't answer—don't go near the door,' I told her. 'Call me back if they keep knocking!'"

"I was ready to jump in the car, but first, I dialed my dad's number at Mr. Payton Williams's house.

"Even though I may have assumed my dad's role as male of the household, out of respect I felt it was my duty to keep him fully informed about everything going on 'back home.'

"The line was busy. I hung up.

"Tanya called back. *'Paul!!'*

"'I'm on my way!' I shouted into the phone.

"I tried my dad's phone two more times. It was still busy. I felt that was somewhat strange, since Dad didn't use the phone much— only to call Tanya, Danglo or me.

"Before heading out I decided to put on my weight gloves in case I needed to use my fists on this man.

"When I arrived at the house, no one was standing in front or anywhere nearby, but an index card had been taped to the front door. I pulled off the card and read the message:

"'Children: Father has passed.'"

Children: Father has passed. Paul repeated the cryptic message to himself as he unlocked the front door and let himself in.

"My first thought was that someone wanted us to know that the priest at St. Rita's church across the street had died. Although we weren't Catholic, we knew the priest.

Tanya was relieved to see her big brother. "He finally went away but not without really banging on the door!" she told him.

"I was still thinking about how strange it was that Dad's phone was busy, so I decided to call the other line at Mr. Payton's house.

"The Williams's daughter answered the phone.

"'What happened?' I asked her.

"I expected the response: 'What are you talking about?' Instead, she said, "He just collapsed."

Wh...? Children: Father has passed.

"Each word of the note now played back to me with new meaning.

"'He passed at 6:09AM,' she was saying."

He. Gerald Vaden. *Children:* **your** *Father has passed.*

"Slowly I put the phone down and broke the news to Tanya. Then I called my brother, Danglo."

Paul learned that his father, who apparently didn't want to wake Mr. Payton or anyone else in the household, had called the paramedics himself.

"The EMT I talked with on the phone said my dad was waiting outside for them and collapsed as soon as they parked the ambulance. They worked on him for several minutes, but he was already in cardiac arrest."

By the time the Williamses learned what had happened, it was too late. It was then that Mr. Payton, Gerald Vaden's surrogate father and long-time friend—not drunk as Tanya had surmised, but in a highly agitated state—had rushed over to the Vaden home to deliver the bad news.

Since it was Sunday and knowing that Gracie Vaden always went to Mt. Erie Baptist Church on Sundays, after knocking several times, Mr. Payton assumed no one was home.

Gerald Vaden was just 51. He'd already had several heart attacks; the last one had occurred in March. He'd been a smoker since he was a kid, so his sudden death was not a total shock to his family and friends. Still, the family wasn't prepared for such a sudden passing.

It was the most difficult day of Paul's young life. Despite the pain and tremendous feeling of loss, Paul knew that as head of the household he had to show the same strength and courage he displayed in the ring. Yet this was different, very different.

"Let me call Mt. Erie and ask someone to get Mom," Paul told Tanya.

The white-uniformed ladies of the church were asked to look for Gracie. When they located her, they asked her to follow them into the church office where she was told of her former husband's passing. Sitting her down, they gave her a glass of water and stayed with her until a friend came to drive her home.

"I guess within the hour the news started to sink in. It was a nightmare, yet I remember how everyone was very supportive."

People came to the house. "Despite my parents' divorce several years earlier, people were there for Mom, my sister, brother and me."

Paul was strong in the presence of his family, attending to their needs and helping with the final arrangements. Yet in his heart, he was hurting.

"I had a fight just three days away, on May 27. I knew I had to be strong, but the pressure was there." Paul decided he had to go into the ring and perform, better than ever before. Quicker, faster and sharper. Speed was his meal ticket, getting his opponent off guard. He would now use it even more effectively. The fight would be dedicated to Gerald Vaden.

"Some people said the fight should have been postponed to give me time to grieve. But I knew I had to do this. He would want me to. Gerald Vaden was no quitter and neither was I."

"My goal now took on new meaning. I remembered how Dad had given me that two week trial when I first went to the Y, and it put a smile on my face. I knew I had given my best as a youngster. Now I was the man of the house, the person in charge and responsible for the family. I wouldn't let him down."

That night Paul fought his heart out, in honor and memory of the man who had helped shape his life.

May 27, 1992 - Landing a nice bodyshot on John Armijo in Paul's 11th pro fight before securing victory after eight rounds

"My uncle, Larry Dixon Sr., was waiting to greet me as I came down the steps of the ring. He asked me after the fight how I was feeling. Without hesitation, I responded, 'I'm hurting.' He asked where and I said, 'in my heart.'"

Reality had set in. The hugs and support from his uncle didn't fill the void left by the death of his father. "He was always there to support me and was at almost all of my bouts. I suddenly realized the totality of it all and it really hurt."

The funeral for Gerald Vaden was well attended by family and friends. Colleagues from Mercy Hospital where he was still employed were among the many mourners present. "Rev. Walter G. Wells, Sr. gave an uplifting eulogy. Charles Ray sang several hymns, including 'How Great Thou Art,' 'Amazing Grace,' and one of my dad's favorite songs, 'Wind Beneath My Wings.'"

Charles had sung at a funeral attended by his dad at Mt. Erie and Gerald liked his voice. Now at his own funeral, Charles sang beautifully.

"Some of the people Dad worked with at Mercy Hospital held a memorial that my mom, Tanya, Danglo and I attended.

"So many people were there… more and more people kept filing into the chapel."

The professional staff as well as his co-workers spoke warmly of him. "It was good that people were nice and came forward and shared with us some lasting memories of Dad. There were tears, of course, but there were joyous moments as we celebrated his life."

Now that his dad's journey on earth was over, Paul felt a sense of calm. "I realize it sounds like a cliché to say this, but I know he's in a better place. I especially like that Dr. Miller was a personal friend of Dad's and he organized a real nice tribute at Mercy. Dr. Miller continued to be very supportive both as a friend and benefactor.

Paul recalled the many times his mom took the kids up to Mercy to see their father and have lunch at the hospital cafeteria. It was always a special treat for them to see him in action with the staff and patients, especially with the kids in the children's ward on the fourth floor.

"Dad would start to whistle as soon as he arrived. Or, sometimes he would sneak into the ward without making a sound, and then: the whistle!

"The kids in the ward knew what would follow. For them, it was magic. The look on the kids' faces said it all. They got to know that whistle."

Paul recalls as a youngster playing with the sick children recuperating from surgery, or the ones who were frequent returning patients because of chronic, or in some cases, acute conditions.

"It took a lot of love and courage for the parents, doctors and general staff to be positive and try not to show fear or anxiety in front of the most challenged patients. When it involved the most vulnerable—the youngest—it took a special person to show strength.

"I got to know some of the kids. I'd play with them, ride the tricycles and play with their toys, never realizing at that young age how fortunate I was that I didn't have a terminal illness. Dad was always smiling, knowing full well that some of these kids were not going to make it. When one of them passed, he'd tell Mom, yet he never cried. But I could see the pain in his eyes."

These memories of his father's devotion to the kids made Paul realize how special his dad was to the hospital staff and its patients.

"After the service I went down to the area where Dad's office was located and touched the door knob as a tribute to him. It was my way of showing him the respect and love he had given to me and others.

"Mercy Hospital was a special place… and it was also the hospital where I was born! I would end up at Mercy whenever I had a doctor's appointment or just to visit Dad.

"Whenever I left the hospital as a kid I always looked up to the eleventh floor as we were waiting for the bus to take us home. Dad always made a point of waving to us."

Following Gerald's death, his mother and Paul went back to Mercy to pick up his final check, clear his locker and gather his belongings. It was a somber and bittersweet final memory of his years at Mercy.

When Paul walked past the familiar bus stop with his mom he was reminded of those earlier years when he had to wait for the bus. Now he was a professional fighter with his own car.

Clutching his car keys, he looked up to the eleventh floor. The familiar smiling face wasn't there anymore. Once again he was overcome by grief as reality swept over him. Things were different now. Life could be so fleeting...

"I helped Mom place his personal items on the back seat, opened the passenger door for her and once more looked up. Getting into the car, I smiled at Mom and started the engine. I was the tough guy, the fighter, yet I was that little kid once again looking up at the man who had molded me so long ago. I can smile and feel good... but it still hurts."

Most of us have experienced the grief that is inevitable when we lose a loved one. What made it even more difficult for Paul was the fact his father's death occurred exactly at the time his career was taking off.

"Stay busy," everyone told Paul, well aware of the deep loss he was feeling. With his ongoing schedule of boxing events, he had plenty to think about. He knew he had to keep his focus. That's what his dad would have advised.

Shortly after his father's death, Paul gained the confidence of Abel Sanchez, a major trainer in the boxing world. "Abel came on the scene just in time. I had been told that I was 'too nice to be a boxer, didn't have the killer instinct and smiled too much!' I honestly didn't give a damn what people thought in that respect. All I cared about was Abel taking my skills to a higher level."

Abel's expertise was legendary in the boxing world. A respected trainer to Terry Norris, he saw in young Vaden a fighter who had talent that needed to be matured. He knew he could make him a champion.

"Our brief union, which lasted from July 1992 to May 1993, made me a fighter that the rest of the boxing world would notice.

"Abel understood that I was motivated, and after my dad's death, rededicated to getting on with my goal. I understood also, having seen Ali in the ring, that much of the general public loved the entertainment spectacle that makes them both love and hate boxing."

Within a few weeks, Abel got Paul to do things differently by showing him how to mold himself into a complete fighter with a quick uppercut from both the right and left hands.

"My training was grueling, yet it started to pay off. I was getting stronger. Abel noticed the difference.

The psychological aspect was a different matter. Abel well understood that like any professional in a public sporting event funded by sponsors, much was demanded. Included in his training, he inspired Paul with stories of the boxers he'd trained.

"In addition to being a great trainer, Abel became a friend. He told me that with my speed, I'd be able to overcome anyone. Anyone! He instilled confidence and was constantly teaching me how to be a professional performer. I was hungry to be the best. Hungry to be the champ. I wanted it more than anything, and I wouldn't disappoint him. I thought of my dad and it made me feel good to know I was doing what he wanted.

Abel was impressed with his young boxer's progress. "He listens and asks questions all the time. Paul is intelligent and doesn't have an attitude."

With Abel Sanchez as his trainer and Bob Fox his sole manager, Paul was now working with two men who were experts in their respective fields.

Fox was an excellent marketer. Paul's trademark, "The Ultimate," was starting to appear at all his bouts on T-Shirts, tank tops, caps and buttons.

The hometown crowd was especially eager to boast of their hero's triumphs and proudly display them whenever he was in the ring.

Timing was good. An important 8-round fight was scheduled the following month in San Diego.

9

Bowling for 160

August 27, 1992. The San Diego Sports Arena. Professional boxer, Paul Vaden matched against Malcolm Shaw of Phoenix.

To a cheering crowd, Paul made his way down the aisle toward the ring. The pre-fight undercards plus the mix of the crowd energized the young fighter as he stepped through the ropes.

As soon as the bell rang, Paul started to move in on his opponent. By the time the sixth round ended, he knew the fight wouldn't last much longer.

Paul Vaden was victorious and scored a TKO in the eighth round. With his hand speed and quick lateral movements, he gave the crowd the performance they came for.

The victory felt good, despite the recent loss of his father. Events such as this one would be another niche that would take him to the top. When he emerged from his dressing room wearing his smart-looking black suit and matching fedora, he looked like a winner.

He was starting to get attention from the females, one in particular. After the fight, Kelly Norris, estranged wife of boxer Terry Norris, came up to Paul to congratulate him. "Great performance! I like the way you fight." Then she quickly added, "I want to talk to you about something."

Terry Norris, the WBC 154 lb. champion, was one of the top three pound-for-pound boxers at the time and a potential opponent in the future.

When Paul didn't respond to Kelly's advances, she suggested, "Let's talk at Garcia's."

Garcia's was a popular San Diego restaurant that was close to the Sports Arena. The crowd usually gravitated to the Mexican restaurant after boxing events.

Paul was curious, and nervous. At Garcia's, the well-wishers were waiting. They swarmed around him, eager to congratulate him on his triumphant win over Shaw.

A few minutes later, Kelly Norris's friend, Stacey came over to him. Sent as a go-between, she sat down and told Paul, "I'm going to be straight with you. Kelly has the hots for you! She's been wanting to approach you since the beginning of the year. Kelly wants your phone number."

Paul looked at Stacey and said nothing. He was feeling very uncomfortable. Stacey added, "I'm going to give you her number."

It had never occurred to Paul that the wife of possibly one of his strongest future opponents wanted to touch base with him. "I'd never paid much attention to her. She was, after all, married. I was focused on my boxing. I was the man of the house and had obligations. I had a lot on my plate and didn't even think of going out and carousing with anyone. My world was boxing."

After a few minutes, Stacey left.

Paul sat there wondering what had just transpired. *What did she want? Was this a setup?*

Suspicious of her intentions, he decided not to call her.

"I walked to my car with Bob Fox. 'You're not going to believe this!' And then I told Bob what had just happened. Bob listened and said nothing.

"The next day after several hours of car shopping, I checked my voicemail. I remember there were eight messages. One was from Kelly—the seventh one. I paged her and she immediately called back.

"Paul, I guess you're wondering why I'm reaching out."

"No." Paul was quick to respond, despite the page he'd sent her. He waited to hear her explanation.

"I've been unhappy for a long time. A long time. I think you can make me smile!" Kelly told him she lived in Alpine, an hour from San Diego. "I want to come to San Diego to meet with you."

They arranged to meet at a parking lot near Nicolosi's, an Italian restaurant.

"I'm feeling a little uncomfortable." Paul was the first to speak.

"Okay," said Kelly, not missing a beat.

After a brief conversation they decided to meet at a bowling alley.

A few days later, Paul was approached by Abel Sanchez. "I want to talk to you, Paul. Someone said they saw you and Mrs. Norris together."

"I'm dating someone from Washington State," said Paul. "She's a model." Paul didn't want to elaborate and explain that Kelly was in touch with him.

Abel looked at Paul. Sanchez was still training Terry.

Within a few days, Paul received a disturbing message on his phone from Terry Norris. Apparently angry that Abel Sanchez was training Paul, his message was both crude and cruel: "That's why your daddy's dead—you're messing with the wrong dude!"

It was upsetting that Terry had to resort to this tactic, but the message tipped the scales for Paul. Until that time, the relationship with Kelly had not been intimate. Paul wanted to be sure of Kelly's intentions before getting more involved. It was she and not he who had made all the advances.

Like anyone, Paul had feelings and eventually wanted to have someone special in his life. Was Kelly the one? She was attractive and available.

Still suspicious of Kelly's intentions, Paul kept asking himself, *"Is she trying to get back at Terry? Is she using me to get to him for his infidelity?"*

Paul Vaden was a 24-year-old man who had never been intimate with a woman. He had concentrated solely on his boxing career.

One evening he met the persistent Kelly Norris at Nicolosi's. "This is for you, handsome." Kelly gave Paul a rose.

"Thank you." The smile on his face masked the surprise of her simple gesture.

"Kelly started to come to the house. I was certainly aware of her intentions. Finally she told me, 'If I can bowl over 160, you have to have sex with me!'

"During the month we spent at the bowling alley, Kelly never scored anywhere near 160. In fact, she never bowled over 130!"

And then it happened. "Kelly scored over 160. We ended up going to the Marriott. From that time on, we used separate cars and met at hotels and my condo. We also started to go out a lot. We'd meet at places like movie theaters where we wouldn't be noticed. I'd enter separately, get a seat, and Kelly would follow me in, looking for me. We would also go into the hotel parking lot with separate cars and enter the room separately. It became a game of cat and mouse for us. We were careful not to be in the public eye."

———————————

"In November of 1992 I was booked for a fight against Sergio Medina at the San Diego Sports Arena. Abel's training had been so good for me. I felt I'd grown so much as a boxer and I was eager for Kelly to be at the fight so I could display my talents in front of her. Kelly said she really wanted to be there for me, but she had to go to Cancun with Terry to a boxing convention that was being held at the same time as the fight.

"I was very upset about this because I knew I was going to give a great performance. And then, a few hours before the fight, I got a call from Kelly. She was at the Dallas airport on her way back from Cancun.

"I'll be there tonight, to see you fight!" she told me excitedly.

"I was beyond elated. The fight went just the way I wanted it to. It was stopped in the second round when Medina sustained a fractured nose, compliments of one of my 'signature uppercuts.' And Kelly was there to see me win!"

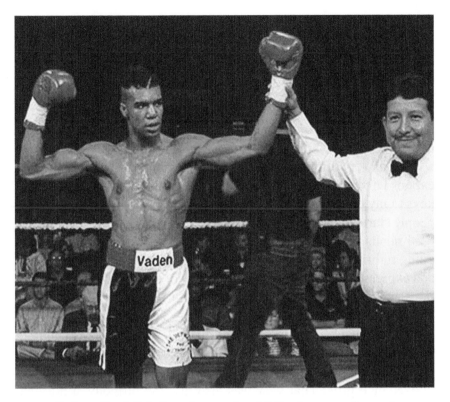

Referee Raul Caiz Sr. raises my hand following second round knockout win over veteran Sergio Medina for 13th professional win at the San Diego Sports Arena

That night after the fight, Paul celebrated with his fans at Garcia's. Terry Norris was also at the restaurant. "I could tell he'd had excessive alcohol intake. I hadn't forgotten that biting phone message he'd left me. There was no love lost between the two of us. What he said about my dad made me want to get back at him."

With such a tense atmosphere, something was bound to happen.

"And then I felt someone bumping into me. I ignored it because the restaurant was crowded. When the bumping happened again and yet again, I turned around. It was Terry."

The two exchanged looks and said little. But looks can say volumes. With a confrontation avoided, it was apparent there was bad blood between the two fighters over Kelly.

"Fortunately Kelly wasn't there, since she'd come to the arena in her own car and didn't go to Garcia's afterward."

"I started to feel more comfortable with Kelly. She told me Terry had moved out, that he'd got someone pregnant.

"I was very romantic—I would write poems and buy her flowers, expensive shoes and gifts. She loved the attention. I gave her the keys to my condo and the garage opener. The relationship grew, and people started talking."

Friends started to inquire, asking if Paul knew what he was doing to himself and his career. Paul's mother wasn't happy either, and expressed her disapproval. She was worried about Kelly's intentions and concerned that Paul would be hurt.

By now the two were a discreet item. Kelly would drive in from Alpine, often meeting him at the bowling alley. With Terry training in the Alpine area at Campo, their meetings became even more frequent.

"Since my birthday is a few days after Christmas, we decided to exchange gifts. That year was also my 25th birthday, a big one. During the time we were together we exchanged expensive bracelets, watches and chains."

Things were going well: his boxing career, a romantic liaison with Kelly… Paul was on top of the world.

10
Reality Check

Terry Norris had recently fired Sanchez, indicating he didn't want to share his training with Paul, an inevitable opponent in his weight class. Terry believed Abel was training Paul to beat him and he didn't hesitate to publicly express his anger.

Whether or not this was the case, Sanchez continued to be impressed with his latest prospect and often commented to others about Paul's dedication to boxing. He liked the young fighter's fortitude and perseverance. "Vaden's uppercut is lethal. He's fast, concise and totally catches his opponent by surprise."

Paul liked the fact that Abel respected his judgment and didn't try to change him. In one of his candid moments, Sanchez said to Paul, "People say you're a prima donna. You ask questions all the time. I tell you—you've got it! You're talented. You're a cool fighter. You're smart and knowledgeable. I don't give a damn who your idol is—if you like Michael Jackson, who cares?! If it works, why not?"

"I enjoyed training with Abel. He had faith in me and he was right: it worked for both of us."

Even though the bond was strong between the two, things were not the same as before after Kelly split with Terry.

"Abel was well aware that I was spending time with Kelly. It was a very uncomfortable situation for him, since he was also the trainer for Terry's older brother, World Champion Orlin Norris.

"On February 24, 1993, I was still with Abel for my first professional fight in Las Vegas, where I registered an impressive third round knockout win over previously undefeated Bryan Isbell.

"After that I had one more fight with Abel as my trainer, on May 6, 1993—a unanimous decision win over Greg Lonon.

"Next on the calendar for Abel and me was a fight the following month in Detroit; but it was not to be. I learned later that Abel had already discussed the Norris/Vaden conflict with my manager, Bob Fox, before sending me a letter telling me of his decision to part ways. I completely understood. He was with Orlin way before I came on the scene.

"Then, shortly after I broke with Abel, things started to unravel with Kelly. Kelly called and suggested we have dinner together before going out dancing. Something was on her mind, she said, and she wanted to talk to me.

"Over dinner she mentioned that Terry was going to sign a big contract with Don King. She said she had to stay in the marriage in order to get a comfortable divorce settlement.

"Then she looked at me, her voice quivering, and blurted out, 'I'm going back to Terry!'"

Paul was shaken by the news. After all the complaints and episodes of apparent disloyalty, Kelly would now leave Paul to return to the same person who had been responsible for so much of her unhappiness!

By late May, Paul knew his relationship with Kelly was over. Terry had found out that Kelly and Paul had gone to Disneyland in April.

"Kelly was scared. Terry was ranting and went ballistic. It was over for us."

As reality sank in, Paul's family and friends became concerned that the abrupt break of the relationship would impact his boxing performance.

"By May 1993, my management team wanted me to get out of San Diego. To add to the chaos, someone broke into my condo and took a box containing very provocative and personal notes that we had written to each other. The local media plus Terry got to see them." Not sure of what to expect and suspicious of Kelly, the decision to leave San Diego resonated well with Paul.

"I decided to drive up to Lakewood, Colorado, where Bob Fox had a home. I had to get things sorted out."

His life had been on a roller coaster, sending him to the highs of his victories in the ring and love for Kelly, and down again to rock bottom, where he was suspicious and hurt.

The decision to go to Colorado was a good one. Before he left, however, he needed to have more confirmation about Kelly's decision to break up. "I'm stubborn and I was hurt, so I decided to call her."

The phone call sealed it.

"When Kelly answered the phone she told me, 'You need to get on with your life.'"

Her tone didn't sit well with Paul. "Kelly was cold and calculating. She made it clear that it was over and she was now with Terry."

On the drive to Colorado, Paul stopped at a few hotels and gave himself a chance to assess his situation. No longer with Kelly and without Abel Sanchez, he knew he had to focus on his career and get his priorities together.

In some bizarre way, the affair with Kelly helped him by molding him into a tougher and more focused boxer. Betrayal, disloyalty and hurt were negatives that he transformed into positive learning experiences. They were grist for the mill, strengthening his determination to keep moving toward his goal of becoming a world boxing champion. He wouldn't look back. He couldn't. He was on his way to fulfill his dream.

11
'I Don't Bite!'

May 24, 1993, was the first anniversary of Gerald Vaden's death. "I was in New Mexico driving on one of the Interstates, preoccupied with thoughts of Dad and never realizing that my speedometer registered 80mph."

Within a few minutes, Paul heard a siren. In the rearview window he saw the flashing lights of the state police. "The officer asked why I was speeding. I told him the truth: I was thinking of Dad, that it was just one year since he passed.

"I'll never forget what happened next. He nodded and told me politely to 'be careful' and let me go."

Paul's time in Colorado proved to be advantageous. Bob Fox encouraged him to go to Flint, Michigan and train with Coach Joe Byrd, Sr., the father of boxer, Chris Byrd.

Chris Byrd, the retired former two-time pro heavyweight champion of the world, was a 1992 Olympic Silver medalist recipient in the middleweight division (165 lbs.). He fought Paul five times in the 156 lbs. class in 1989 and 1990, with Paul winning three of the five bouts.

"Christopher became a close friend and eventually my best friend." Christopher's first child, Jordan Christine Byrd became Paul Vaden's goddaughter and when Paul's son was born, he was named Dayne Christopher, a tribute to his good friend.

Coach Byrd was the head coach of the 1992 U.S. Olympic Boxing team. He had been Paul's coach in 1989 during the World Amateur Championships in Moscow. He also became the 1990 Goodwill Games coach in which Paul had participated. Joe Byrd, Sr., was his son's coach throughout his boxing career, from amateur to the professional level. Coach Byrd set out to get Paul into prime shape.

Paul's stay in Flint was very productive. "The Byrds were like family; they really made me feel at home. I knew that eventually I had to return to San Diego, but this time away was valuable to train and reflect. I also needed to get my bearings after having gone through so much.

"I remained in Flint from July to December of 1993. I was training hard and ready for my next bout, scheduled in Las Vegas on December 18, 1993."

Paul won the fight against veteran boxer Randy Smith but was soon sidelined with a bout of chicken pox. "I ended up at my mom's, who nursed me back to health."

At the beginning of 1994, Arnie Rosenthal, a music lover who occasionally dabbled as a singer, started talking to Paul.

"Arnie, who was known as 'Tokyo,' called often. He knew the business end of boxing that Bob Fox didn't. Starting in 1992 when I first met him, Arnie was my boxing matchmaker."

Rosenthal, who was formerly the President of Financial News Network (FNN) TV, had an extensive music background. Their mutual taste in music and entertainment created a natural bond between the two. It didn't take long for Paul to decide to ask Arnie to be his manager.

"Arnie is a highly acclaimed recording artist. He was there with me during my tenure with Abel Sanchez."

Arnie knew the best thing for Paul would be to start training in Vegas, far from any temptations that could cause a possible setback.

"In the meantime, Arnie was in talks with the promoter of John Montes and my potential challenger for the vacant IBF Intercontinental Junior Middleweight title. Montes was a tough fighter who was rated #7 by the IBF. It was supposed to be a tough match for me. In fact, several of the experts thought I was in over my head. Montes had a record of 43 wins, 5 losses with an impressive 30 knockouts."

Vaden, who was rated #10 in 1994 by the same IBF, knew this would be a major event. "I was 18-0 at the time. This was to be my first 12-round fight. In fact, I never even had a scheduled 10-

round fight before the Montes match. I went from an 8-round fighter straight to the maximum limit of 12 rounds."

March 25, 1994 was the date set for the match in Vegas. Eddie Mustafa Muhammad was Paul's trainer. Muhammad, previously Eddie Gregory, was a respected ex-boxer who was the former light heavyweight champion of the world. He had the expertise and knowledge of someone who had been through the rigors of both ends of the sport as a professional boxer and now as a trainer.

"Eddie had inspired me when I was a kid when I read about him in *The Ring* magazine. Eddie's stable consisted of Skipper Kelp, Emmett Linton Jr., Frank and Thomas Tate, and several other boxers. They believed in me and wanted me to succeed.

"Mike McCallum, a former three division world champion, had seen me spar and one day when I was at a car wash, Mike was there also. He made a point of coming over to me. 'You can fight your ass off. You'll go far,' he told me. I knew he meant it and an endorsement from someone like McCallum carried considerable weight.

"I was training hard, back in my element. I thought of Kelly, of course, but I refused to let it interfere with my goal."

Fox Sports sponsored the event on *Prime Ticket*. Even though Abel Sanchez no longer worked with him, Paul still sought his counsel and expertise. "Abel gave me the rundown on Montes. He told me he was a veteran and a tremendous body puncher." Abel also told him that Montes was vulnerable to uppercuts, a Vaden trademark.

Abel smiled at Paul. "I believe you know how to throw those!" The uppercut, made famous by Vaden, could be the undoing of Montes and Abel wanted to make sure Paul was aware of it.

Abel was a steady and reliable person for gathering sound advice about upcoming boxing opponents. "During my time with him and even following our split, I'd always ask him for an appraisal of my challengers.

"'How long will it take me?' I'd ask him. Meaning: how many rounds would it take to knock out or stop my opponents? Abel was always honest with me. Because of my ability to inflict damage with my uppercuts, combined with my hand speed, opponents were having a difficult time lasting in the ring. Abel also indicated that he expected Montes to go to the late rounds."

Montes came out in the first round, swarming Paul to the ropes with hard body shots. "None of them were hurting me. I waited patiently, picking his shots. Then I perfectly timed his body shot, landing a short yet very quick right uppercut. He was hurt. He survived the round but he was never the same. I won an easy 12-round unanimous decision. My speed, stamina and size overwhelmed him. He would retire following this defeat."

Paul Vaden stunned his critics and the boxing world and emerged triumphant. Of the scheduled 12-round event, he dropped his opponent, John Montes, in the third round! It was Paul's moment to shine. He had the IBF belt!

"My mom, sister, Larry Dixon Jr., Robert Coons, Tom Mustin, Skipper Kelp, Emmett Linton, Jr. and several family and friends had traveled from all over to support me." Sharing the win with his family and the team that was with him from the start as a youngster at the Jackie Robinson YMCA, meant so much to the new champion.

March 25,1994 - Hugging my Aunt Roberta Houston as Mom looks on at the Post-Fight Party after defeating John Montes in Las Vegas, NV, moving undefeated record to 19 wins 0 losses

Now wearing the belt as the IBF champ with the media and sportscasters taking photos and interviewing him, Paul remembered his dream. He was suddenly back in his hometown thinking of the times he would steadfastly show up at the Y and practice.

It had all come home for him. The title was his and he was at the top of world. "I felt good. It was decided that I should go for the world title within a year. Mark Stewart had come aboard as my promoter. I stayed in Vegas and began training hard again."

Paul's opponent, Jason Papillon, was a respected fighter from Broussard, Louisiana. The event was held in Atlantic City, New Jersey, on June 30 and Paul won by unanimous decision in a 12-round fight. Papillon was a formidable opponent and an undefeated southpaw.

"Jason had hit me. It was in the 11th round. I was hurt, but I was determined to weather the storm and the results came in the 12th and final round.

"I was staggered by Jason in the 11th round. I knew I had to finish strong in the final 12th round. I was far ahead on the scorecards, but I didn't want to leave the impression or claim from anyone that given a few more rounds, he could have dominated me. Instead, I dominated the 12th. I answered the bell and won."

After the fight, Paul went to Babylon, Long Island where he had family. "My Uncle Ron owned two McDonald's, one at Pitkin Avenue in Brooklyn and the other in Flushing, Queens. I had elevated Ron to 'uncle' status, his former wife, Bernadette (Mrs. 'C') as my 'aunt' and his kids, Ronnie, Ryan and daughter Evi as 'cousins.' They may not have been blood relatives, but they were there for me, and they were family. Just because someone isn't blood related doesn't mean I can't treat them like family. I was grateful to have such an extended family.

"A beautiful gesture from my Uncle Ron was the autograph signing they arranged for me at the local McDonald's. I was amazed at the number of people who showed up."

Paul was especially appreciative that despite the city's searing summer heat and humidity, so many young people eagerly waited in line to get an autographed picture of the "The Ultimate."

"The response from the people in both Brooklyn and in Flushing, Queens was inspiring." Paul was beginning to realize that he was no longer just a hometown boy but someone who had become nationally—even internationally recognized.

In August 1994, Paul returned to live in San Diego and started training hard at Murphy's Boxing Gym. With a ranking by all three major sanctioning bodies after the Montes fight, he was ranked #4 after his win over Papillon.

Joking around with the late Charles Miller, M.D., family friend and longtime supporter, after having lunch

By the end of 1994, Paul was ranked #2 by the IBF. This was a notable accomplishment, given the fact that he wasn't promoted by the three major boxing moguls, Don King, Bob Arum, and "Main Events" of the Duva family.

With renewed confidence, Paul started preparing for his next event, another Vegas venue at the Flamingo Hilton, against Heriberto Valdez. "It was a scheduled 10-round non-title fight. I weighed in at 153½ lbs. Valdez weighed in at 168 lbs. In most cases, this fight would have been canceled, as the contract weight for the fight was 158 lbs."

Yet the fight would be held. Paul's superior skills and boxing IQ would prove to be an advantage.

"It was the main event and like most Vegas fights, attracted a good crowd." The fight result was a TKO in the 6th round, another niche in his belt.

"I moved away from thinking about Kelly. Instead, I concentrated on my boxing routine and started dating other women. Life has its ups and downs, but I was starting to see sunshine ahead. Before long, I had signed for another boxing match, this time in New Orleans, Louisiana.

"On March 12, I left for New Orleans with Carl Blakenship, my videographer. In 1976 at the Jackie Robinson YMCA, Carl was one of my first boxing instructors and he'd gone on to have a career in video and computer production. In 1990 during my U.S. team days as an amateur and throughout most of my professional career, Carl became my personal videographer and thus, part of my boxing entourage that traveled to events with me.

"En route to New Orleans we had a stop at the Houston Airport. While we were waiting to board the next plane, I phoned the late Doris Welch, a lifelong family friend living in the Houston area. It was my ritual to call Doris, whom we fondly called 'Nanny,' whenever I had to change flights in Houston.

"Because of the call to Nanny, I was the last person on the plane for the short flight to New Orleans. I remember I had my title belt with me in a special suitcase and I was wearing a 'newsboy' cap.

"As I sat down in the aisle seat and buckled up, I noticed someone directly across the way in the aisle seat. Then I took a second look. *What a beautiful girl!*

"I wanted to speak to her in the worst way. I had to say something to her!" He decided the best approach would be to do something bold and totally out of character. He would write her a note and introduce himself.

"I asked the person next to me on the window seat for a pen and paper and proceeded to write: 'My name is Paul Vaden. I will soon be the Junior Middleweight Champion of the World. Your beauty is positively distracting me. Are you married or do you have a boyfriend? If not, how about being my guest and watching me perform in New Orleans?'"

Paul proceeded to write his pager and phone number on the note. Although he didn't give it to her, he continued to try to connect with her. Unfortunately, she was wearing headsets, so was unaware of his advances.

The plane taxied to the gate and Paul stayed on while people scrambled to retrieve their carry-on bags from the overhead bins. He was nervous, having never made such a bold move. Yet somehow it felt normal, or at least acceptable.

"As I was about to disembark, I gave the note to Carl and asked him to deliver it for me."

In the terminal Paul stopped at the restroom and then proceeded to the baggage claim where he met Carl, who confirmed that he'd delivered Paul's note.

"As I headed over toward the baggage cartel, I felt a nudge at my elbow. 'I don't bite,' she smiled.

"After collecting her luggage, she gave me her business card. I learned that her name was Lisa Marie Cornin. She lived in Austin and was connecting in Houston on her way to her former hometown, New Orleans, to spend time with her parents."

Paul told her of his upcoming bout in New Orleans and asked her if she would attend.

"I don't like looking at boxing events," she confessed.

Paul was not about to be put off. "This one will be televised. You'll be able to see it on TV."

"Good! Then I'll probably watch it!"

After he had collected his bags, Paul thanked Carl for serving as his messenger. "I think I just found my wife!"

Carl gave him a smile and a rather strange look.

Before the fight, Paul's mom usually led the group in a prayer. It was a routine that Paul welcomed and that helped him prepare for the performance.

The Crescent City crowd was eager to see the event. They would witness the young pugilist at his best, with a TKO in the sixth round against Andreas Arellano. And Lisa Marie Cornin did indeed watch the fight on TV, sponsored by USA Network.

With another impressive win, Paul headed back to San Diego. "Once I got back home, I spoke on the phone daily with Lisa." He learned that she was also a professional, with a career in pharmaceuticals. "I invited her to come out to San Diego from her home in Austin. I felt this would give us a chance to get to know each other and also, Lisa could meet my mom and the rest of the family."

Lisa flew to San Diego over Easter weekend and stayed at Paul's condo. "The first thing we had to do, Lisa said, was go to Starbucks! She loved Starbucks' grande non-fat latte with two substitute sugar sweeteners. I guess I had a few things to learn! Lisa told me her Starbucks latte was a daily ritual."

Paul was a perfect gentleman, giving Lisa a two-day visit to remember. During the weekend they enjoyed long conversations and learned a great deal about each other.

"I found it ironic that my idol, Michael Jackson, was married to another Lisa Marie—Lisa Marie Presley! My friends got a kick out of this too!"

Paul showed her many of the most famous scenic spots of the area: the Pacific Ocean and bluffs along the California coast, Rose Canyon, and a view of Mt. Soledad from the Top of the Cove restaurant where they dined on the first evening.

On Easter Sunday Paul took Lisa on a brunch cruise of the harbor. Despite his ferocity in the boxing ring, Lisa realized that Paul could be a charmer. He was a very kind, considerate, highly sensitive person. The two days were magical.

While they were driving through the city's historic Balboa Park and Paul was pointing out its Spanish mission-style architecture, Lisa turned to him and said with a smile, "You know I'm not averse to going to McDonald's too!"

It was all Paul needed. She was indeed a good prospect that he didn't want to lose. His instinct from day one when they met on the airplane was starting to play out. He knew she was the one for him.

12
You're All I See

On April 29, Paul flew to Austin to visit Lisa in her adopted hometown. "We ate at Pappasito's, a famous Mexican restaurant. With the domed capital of the Lone Star State in the background, it was a nice respite from the hectic training I was into daily. However, I did manage to do a workout in Austin, mindful of what was to come."

The next day was a boxing event in Landover, Maryland between Simon Brown and Vincent Pettway. "I was too busy with Lisa to watch the Pettway-Brown fight. My strength and conditioning coach, Yogi Najera, watched it for me and gave me a thorough report. Lisa had all my attention."

Pettway knocked out Brown in the 6th round, but Pettway was put on the canvas twice by Brown. "The fight was important because my own match against Pettway would soon be scheduled. I knew I'd be the underdog in the match, but I'd use my ring smarts, speed and size to overcome him.

"When I watched the knockout later, I had to admit that it was one of the most chilling knockouts I'd ever seen—and Brown had a reputation as a boxer impossible to knock out!"

Paul's next fight was in Atlantic City, New Jersey, on May 16, 1995, in a match with Reuben Bell. Bell was under the Duva "Main Events Promotions" umbrella.

As an undefeated boxer, Paul knew it would be a fight that would challenge him to the utmost. Televised as the *Tuesday Night Fights* on USA Network, it was a mandatory bout in order to move onto the world title fight.

"I should have cancelled the fight. I had a bad cold and was still sick when I arrived in New Jersey. Although a non-title fight, it was an important one for me. Bell traded insults and I was in no mood to humor him.

"I also remember getting a call from a female reporter on the upcoming fight. She was calling from Washington, D.C., Bell's hometown, and was very quick to relate to me how confident Bell was—that he was certain he would emerge the winner. She indicated that Bell thought I was overrated and vulnerable; therefore he was going to knock me out (!)

"She then asked for my thoughts. I told her I'd see him in the ring Tuesday night and he would get every opportunity to express himself in person."

It would be an event that would cause the boxing world, from the writers to the pundits, to take notice. "I had watched tapes of Bell in previous fights. I studied his moves and looked at his stance and his activity.

"As fate would have it, an article appeared by Jerry Magee in my hometown paper, the *San Diego Union Tribune.* He'd asked me a lot of questions. A lot. I thought nothing of it and had answered in my best and most frank way. The day of the fight the article was printed. It wasn't flattering. Magee wrote: "'Ultimate Fighter' or a 'Flash in the Pan?' Is he a prima donna thinking he's Michael Jackson?'"

Paul was aware of the sports writers' lack of coverage for him. As the real deal—a born and bred San Diegan—he had never received respect from the local media. This was something Paul couldn't understand.

"I got up each day at 4 AM to get in my running. I pleaded for extra rounds during sparring sessions. I worked boxing mitts with my trainer for 45 minutes straight through the bell while wearing a wetsuit, with no rest. Some prima donna!"

Despite his lingering cold and its symptoms, Paul was determined to step into the ring against Bell. Also, Lisa was able to attend the fight. Her presence helped enormously. Paul's motivation to make the event a "must win" made it all the more important.

The East Coast fight drew a Bell-friendly crowd. Many of his fans had made the trip from D.C. to Atlantic City to see their hometown fighter in action. The crowd made Vaden even more determined to give them a surprise.

Hit hard by Bell in the second round, Paul quickly recovered. He was confident it wouldn't be long before he'd land his signature punch—the uppercut on the much shorter Bell. Despite being hit in the second round, Paul was able to use his skill of lateral movement to keep Bell at bay.

One round later, he turned the entire fight around, connecting with some brutal uppercuts and putting together quick multi-punch combinations. Bell would never recover from this onslaught. From the third and subsequent rounds, he would become a step and a half behind Paul's punches. He was also getting increasingly winded. As usual, Paul was getting stronger by the round.

Round after round, he stayed the course and by the decisive 10th round, Paul had the officials in his corner. He won by decision and, despite the ongoing and agonizing effects of a bad cold, proved himself to be the number one mandatory contender to face Pettway for the IBF World Junior Middleweight Championship.

"I returned to the dressing room, showered and met Lisa. We headed out to one of the many restaurants on the boardwalk. Over dinner, Lisa indicated that she was seriously thinking of transferring to San Diego. My mom liked her. My team liked her. And so did I!" Seeing her off at the airport, they both knew their relationship was now solid.

In July Lisa moved to the Simi Valley town of Sunnyvale, not far from San Jose and a mere one-and-a-half hour flight from San Diego.

"Lisa would fly to San Diego on the weekends or I would occasionally go to Sunnyvale. Because of my training regimen, it was easier for her to make the flight down to see me. Lisa's company's management reassured her she could transfer to San Diego by early 1996."

Paul Vaden, a focused and determined fighter in the ring, proved equally adept at arranging an important moment in his life. "I knew I wanted to ask Lisa to marry me and I didn't want to wait much longer. Her birthday weekend was July 29, so we made plans to celebrate in San Diego. I reserved a hotel suite at the Torrey Pines Hilton where we would also have dinner.

"When Lisa was still living in Austin, we visited a jewelry store where we'd looked at diamond ring settings and Lisa had chosen one she liked. I called the jewelry store. The saleswoman, Jessica, remembered me and said that she would ship the ring via UPS."

In the meantime, Paul had been training hard, knowing full well after the fight with Reuben Bell that he had to be in the ring soon for the title fight. It was a perfect time to ask Lisa to marry him.

"I had signed with Don King Promotions. I sustained a bad bruise on my right hand which my doctor checked out. He wanted me to get an X-ray. I told him, fractured or not, I was fighting! I'd waited my whole life for this opportunity. It may never come again. 'I'm fighting, I'm fighting!'"

Given the okay by his medical staff, Paul's thoughts turned to Lisa and the big day. "A few days before Lisa would be here, the ring still hadn't arrived—very upsetting! Apparently, there was a problem with the audio at the gate entry of my condo. I called back and it was finally delivered to me on Friday."

The Torrey Pines Hilton restaurant had a live band and Paul knew the musicians. The late Shep Myers, Paul's friend, was the pianist. "During dinner I asked Shep to play 'Happy Birthday.' Lisa loved it!"

After a wonderful dinner and tribute to his soon-to-be fiancée, they retired to their hotel suite.

"Underneath the bed I'd hidden the ring. The radio coincidently was playing, 'I've Been Waiting for a Girl Like You!'

"I asked Lisa to come out to the balcony."

The night was perfect, brilliant stars and a large moon casting a romantic setting for what would transpire.

"I'd written a poem for Lisa titled 'You're All I See,' that ended with the words, 'Will you marry me?'"

Lisa was smitten and readily accepted Paul's marriage proposal. The first person they called to convey the good news about their engagement was Gracie Vaden.

Everyone was very happy for the couple. Paul realized he was entering into a meaningful and enduring relationship with a woman he loved. Lisa was not someone who was out to use him, but a woman who cared deeply for him, who would be moving to his hometown to be with him. She would be his biggest supporter in his quest to get to the top.

Excited as she was about the engagement and their future together, Lisa fully understood how important it was for Paul to stay focused on the big event that would take place on August 12 in Las Vegas, Nevada, when he would face the formidable Pettway. Like everyone who'd followed Paul's meteoric rise to the top, she knew this was the premiere title fight, the one he'd dreamed of.

All the years of training… the Jackie Robinson Y, the "Chitlin Circuit" road trips with "Betsy," the rickety old bus… the musty old motels… the grueling workouts and training routine… all of it was well worth it, Paul declared when he reminisced with her. He was so ready to fulfill the dream of that four year old standing in front of the TV and seeing Paul Vaden in the ring instead of Muhammad Ali, with the crowds cheering his latest victory…

With the late Jorge Gonzalez, Assistant Trainer, and David Love, Head Trainer, following final boxing rehearsals in San Diego one week before world title encounter with Champion Vincent Pettway... I'm ready!!

13
The Walk

Las Vegas. The place to escape. Sin City. The City of Lights. From all corners of the world, regardless of the time of year, big city spenders, naïve first-time gamblers and curious coupon clippers stream into the city's casinos, hotels, bars and restaurants. With entertainers from every venue giving their 5-star performances along the world-famed Strip, Vegas gives everyone a chance to lose themselves in the myriad of glitz and neon.

Vegas is also the city where titles are bestowed on some of the world's greatest athletes. Nowhere is that skill so colorfully witnessed as in a ringside seat at a world championship boxing event.

Boxing is raw entertainment, nothing rehearsed, and no way of predicting the outcome. The objective is to catch one's opponent off guard and go for his perceived weakness.

With a different scenario at each performance, boxing offers its spectators a full range of chills and thrills. With each round the script changes, forcing each corner to strategize their next move. All eyes are riveted on the two performers in the ring, on their every move. In boxing anything can happen and it often does.

Whether live, on TV or the big screen, major boxing events drew millions of fans eager to witness history in the making when a new champ was crowned.

The stakes were even higher when it was the seminal event of a boxer's career. Would he make it to the top or not? One-on-one, mano-a-mano, championship fights captured the attention of the world's greatest sportscasters, reporters and fans throughout the world. Everyone loved a championship fight!

For the athletes, after weeks of intense training, finally it all came down to that single Big Event that would take place for Paul Vaden in Vegas.

On August 12, 1995, Paul Vaden would experience the culmination of a young San Diego boy's dream. It was the moment in his career toward which he had worked with such diligence and dedication. Unless they'd been through it themselves, few people could appreciate the sacrifice and self-discipline required for any performer—athlete, actor, musician, magician, comedian—to compete at the highest level.

The boxer's crown is not a glittering headpiece bestowed through royal bloodline or political appointment. It is a titled belt that pays tribute to hundreds of hours of work, unrivaled courage and a mindset trained to focus on timing, precision and delivery.

The match was booked at Vegas's prestigious MGM Grand Hotel and Casino and would be televised on Showtime Network. Seating 16,800, with its state-of-the art acoustics, special lighting and sound, the MGM was a favorite venue for championship boxing events. Spectators were already anticipating the crowning of the new king of the world junior middleweight title.

"I stayed up late the night before the fight," says Paul. "This is a habit of mine. I envisioned the entire process from start to finish in my mind, making me prepared for any eventuality. I was ready for Pettway. Still considered the underdog by the boxing world, I would use my unique speed, smarts, stamina, dangerous uppercuts, and trust in myself."

In the hotel room before the fight, 40 family members and close friends had assembled to wish Paul well. Paul's mother, Gracie Vaden, delivered her traditional prayer, this time taking on a different and more poignant significance. Aware of the historic bout about to convene, Gracie invoked some memorable words: "Fulfill the dream the little boy has had since he was eight years old. This is the realization of his dream, Lord."

"When I remembered my third grade speech to my elementary school class announcing that I wanted to be a world boxing champion, tears came to my eyes. This would be the first time I cried before a fight. I'd never been so emotional during one of my mom's traditional prayers."

Paul's entry into the ring was that of a triumphant performer coming home to throngs of loyal fans. His chief sparring partner and cousin, Larry Dixon, Jr., remarked: "You're the true first one from the city of San Diego to get this far, so you've already made history. You're the first!"

"Larry was right, but that wasn't enough. My script had to end with a belt around my waist! I looked at my brother, Danglo—I'd never seen him so nervous—and proceeded out of my dressing room.

"The last encouraging words I heard from my dressing room were from Mike Tyson, who remarked, 'Good luck, Paul, it's your night!' I was so focused, I just stared at the champ and nodded."

Paul knew so much rode on this one fight. It was his to make or break.

Toni Leonard, Sugar Ray's sister-in-law, made his outfit. "I wore a 'Michael Jackson-inspired' jacket—yes, it was more of a jacket than the familiar robe that boxers usually wear when entering the ring. True to the Jackson image, it was a gold jacket with epaulettes and gold sequins.

"To complete the outfit, I had black trunks with matching striped gold sequins. These were the colors of our original Jackie Robinson YMCA boxing team. I was conscious that I represented the people of my city, from my family to the individuals who were there for me along the way. I wouldn't forget them. The outfit made quite a statement as I entered the ring. "

That walk from the dressing room to the ring was a walk for everyone who had participated in the evolution of Paul Vaden. Family, friends, managers, trainers, all were part of the event. Paul was thinking about these people, but most of all he was thinking about his absent father and wishing he could be there to see him arrive at the pinnacle of his long quest to the top.

"'This is the walk!'" shouted my manager, Arnie "Tokyo" Rosenthal, as my team and I started to make our way down the aisle toward the ring." Tokyo understood the significance of the moment coupled with Vaden's passion for the theatrical. It was, indeed, his moment to perform. It had all come down to this.

At the point where Paul was ready to enter the ring, the audio played the rap song, "The Ultimate Show." Performed by local San Diegan rapper and longtime friend, Andrew Rayford, it was a fitting touch, choreographed perfectly as the young boxer stepped into the ring with his entourage to the cheers of his fans. This was what he had waited for. It was his moment.

At last he would join the pantheon of heroes in the boxing world. This was indeed "the walk"—a walk into history and the fulfillment of years of hard work and commitment.

Paul's strategy was carefully worked out. "My methodology was to overwhelm Pettway with my speed, smarts and size. I figured these intangibles would wear him down. I would remain steadfast and focused on my plan. Also, I thought he might be overconfident." Given the fact that he was the underdog going into the ring and that he had knocked out Brown, added to Pettway's perceived overconfidence against Vaden.

"I didn't care if the crowd wasn't as engaged in the early rounds. This was MY story. I was the one who needed to be triumphant. Those were the dangerous rounds, the early ones. Table setters for me, so to speak. But if I remained disciplined to my script, in the end they would be cheering for a curtain call."

The fight started slowly, with both boxers cautious. After several rounds, however, the Vaden technique started to show results.

**August 12, 1995 - Just finished landing a flush right hand (sound familiar?)
on Champion Vincent Pettway in the late rounds of our
World Junior Middleweight Title Fight at The MGM Grand Hotel
and Casino in Las Vegas, NV**

In the 9th round Paul made significant inroads. The next two rounds were also strong. In his corner, David Love, his head trainer, as well as Jorge Gonzalez, his assistant trainer and veteran trainer, Jimmy Montoya, were all pleased at the progress of the fight. "They didn't want me to take my foot off the pedal."

As the bell for the 12th and final round was about to ring, Montoya said, "Paul, this is the three minutes of the rest of your life. Fight it like that."

The final round found Paul moving around and getting the right moment to get to Pettway. With 27 seconds left, Paul hit him with a right hand up against the ropes—a classic right uppercut that was vintage Vaden. The referee Richard Steele called it. It was over! Paul Vaden, by a TKO in the 12th round, became the IBF Champion of the world!

It was the turning point in Paul's life, the greatest of his fights—the fight in which the boxing world, like it or not, would have to recognize its new champion. Paul Vaden had finally arrived.

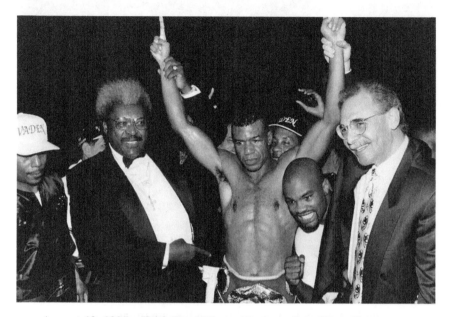

August 12, 1995 – With David Love, Trainer; Don King, Promoter; Cousin Larry Dixon, Jr.; and Arnie "Tokyo' Rosenthal, Manager; following upset 12th round TKO win over Vincent Pettway to capture world junior middleweight crown

A pivotal moment in life, Paul Vaden's name would be entered into the hallmark of the boxing world. The energy he brought to the ring that night raised his standard to the highest. His uncompromising nature made him a dynamo to contend with, forcing his opponent to take notice.

Paul's compelling drama in the boxing ring would continue now that he had the belt. Meticulous and unwavering, he stayed the course. The results were a new world champ.

The euphoria of the moment soon resonated with cheers and hugs from Paul's trainers. Soon his mother entered the ring, accompanied by another round of cheers. The triumphant champion was glowing.

The post-fight press conference gave Paul an opportunity to thank the people who had been with him through the years. Present to witness his big moment were Gracie Vaden, his mom; trainers; promoters; Don King; and Lisa, who Paul introduced to the press as "the First Lady of the World Junior Middleweight champ."

"I remember telling the press that having a woman in my life made all the difference. It felt so good not having to be in a clandestine relationship. For the first time I could shout to the world that I was in love, and I have that person here with me. What a feeling! Think about it. I chose to propose two weeks before the biggest fight of my life and I had just accomplished my lifelong dream!

"I know my strategy worked—I wore out Pettway. Dr. Ferdie Pacheco's post-fight analysis was right on target. He said that I was 'obviously a very talented, quick-handed smart fighter, in shape, who does things on his own time.'" Coming from the seasoned sportscaster who was a longtime cornerman of Paul's idol, Ali, and who had seen so many fights in his lifetime, the tribute to Paul was sharp and concise. Pacheco had seen fighters come and go and he knew that Paul Vaden had given the boxing world a solid champ.

In San Diego the local paper placed Paul's triumphant victory on the sports page in section C-8. No front page accolade for the native real deal. Paul was aware of this apparent snub and didn't take kindly to it.

"I became the first and, to this date, only native San Diegan ever to capture a professional world boxing title." Yet his home city from the mayor's office to the sports writers, refused to give credence to its significance.

But facts are facts. Paul Vaden was the world champion. He had achieved his goal.

**"It's Happened"! With my new world title belt and gold sequined
garb during a photo shoot for *The Ring* magazine**

On August 18 the brand new title belt arrived by Federal Express.
The champ knew what he had to do next. The city may have overlooked the importance of the event, but Paul's journey to the top
needed one more important stop.

"I went to my father's grave at Mt. Hope Cemetery. I raised the
belt high over my head, displaying it proudly for him. Tears started
welling up in my eyes. I remember saying, 'Thank you for your support, belief in me, and for teaching me right from wrong.' I know
he was saying, 'My boy did it again! His dream was fulfilled and he
got the job done!'"

It was a poignant moment for the new champion... his personal way of telling his dad how much he appreciated what he'd done for him, and that he would never, ever forget all the bad as well as the good times that had taken him to the top. Paul knew he couldn't have done it without the strength, love and support he'd received from his parents.

He felt blessed, even though he knew he would soon be tested again in the spotlight. Right now, that didn't matter. That would come later. It was time to give thanks to those who never wavered and who gave that young kid a chance to attain his goal. It was good, all good—yet so incomplete without the physical presence of the one person who had done so much for him.

14
Nemesis

Paul Vaden, the IBF world champion, was enjoying his time in the sun. He had attained his overall goal in life, was engaged to a beautiful woman and at the pinnacle of his game.

Amidst the glory, Paul remembers saying, "The more blessed you are, the nicer you should be." He was well aware that with fame came even closer scrutiny of one's character.

"The Ultimate" had remained humble in his moment of victory. He recalled the boxer, Shane Mosley, a former U. S. teammate, approaching him and asking, "What was it like?"

At that time Shane's career hadn't taken off yet. Later Shane would become a superstar and multi-division pro boxing world champion.

Shane's question was subjective. He knew that a world champion belt came with distinction. It was a unique honor that placed a person in a special position. Likewise, Paul realized he had arrived at a peak moment in his career that would be emulated by many others.

Success and fame had bestowed on the young boxer a sense of pride coupled with a desire to share his dream with others. It had been a long climb and like most task-oriented people, even though he had realized his goal, he was aware that it came with a price. He knew he was expendable in the boxing world and that soon someone would be there to challenge him. For the moment, however, he could take pride in the fact that he had achieved his goal. He had a right to gloat and be proud.

"I also got an important phone call after the fight, from Sugar Ray Leonard. It was a title-winning congratulatory phone call from the champ. Ray told me he'd watched my fight and was impressed with my patience—not letting the crowd lure me out of my style. Ray told me I was a very smart fighter. He also congratulated me on my engagement and pending marriage.

"Everything had come full circle! I started boxing in 1976, the same year Ray was creating magic at the Summer Olympics in Montreal. Like Ali and Michael Jackson, Ray had always been one of my icons. And now he was calling me!

"I dreamed this would happen, and now it had!"

In the weeks that followed his great triumph, Paul bonded with his family and Lisa.

"On Labor Day, Lisa and I drove to her place in San Jose and I stayed with her until the end of the month.

"I knew I'd be in the ring again soon. The boxing world wanted another match. It wasn't about to let the new champion have much time to himself. Sure enough, while I was in San Jose, Arnie Rosenthal called to inform me that the next fight would be against Terry Norris."

Press Conference in New York, NY to announce the World Junior Middleweight Title Unification match between Paul Vaden & Terry Norris

Terry! Paul was well aware that one of these days he'd be facing Norris. Don King was itching for this match. Big money was at stake and the boxing public wanted this fight soon.

"Scheduled for November 4, 1995, the fight would be sponsored by Fox TV at the MGM Hotel and Casino in Las Vegas. I was told that a press conference/ photo op would be held at the famed steak joint, Gallagher's on West 52nd Street in New York."

Paul took the Red Eye to New York where he had a reservation at the Novotel, adjacent to Gallagher's.

The people in both camps knew of Kelly's affair with Paul, yet the subject was taboo. No one would mention it, even though the two fighters were aware of the tension, evident from the moment they saw each other to do the classic "stare down" photo that appeared in the *New York Post* and *New York Daily News.* The photo of the two showed both fighters in gladiator pose, determined and focused, staring at each other without flinching.

"I immediately returned to San Diego and started training for what would be a major fight in November to unify the IBF and WBC belts." As part of the training, Paul had to lose 25 lbs. He already knew the fitness training procedure; he'd been through it many times before: dieting, running and sparring. Training for this fight would take on an added dimension with the circumstances surrounding the Kelly episode. It would test him to the max, but he was up for the challenge.

"The final press conference before the fight was on November 2 at the MGM Grand. The main event would be a fight between Mike Tyson and Buster Mathis, Jr. In 1992, Tyson had been convicted of raping Desiree Washington and sentenced to six years in prison, but was released after serving only three years. The Las Vegas event was to be Tyson's second comeback fight. The boxing public was waiting to see if "Iron Mike" was still at his prime. Excitement was high."

Then the unimaginable happened. "I had just arrived from my second to last workout before the fight, settled into my hotel suite and turned on the TV. That's when I saw the news flash on ESPN that Tyson had sustained a fractured thumb. Arnie called to tell me the whole event, including my fight with Terry Norris, had been cancelled."

This situation changed everything.

"I never believed Mike Tyson fractured his thumb. They said it happened during a sparring session, but why would he be sparring two days before a fight? And if Tyson really did sustain a fracture, I found it odd that Don King would eventually reschedule a fight about 45 days later, considering the colossal amount of money invested in Tyson's return.

"I think Don King was being ultra-cautious about Mike's journey back, so what I really believe this 'delay' was all about was the rivalry of a same-day event that would happen right down the street.

It was the famous 'Rubber Match' between heavyweights Evander Holyfield and Riddick Bowe. Their first encounters had been action-packed and were box office sell-outs. They were both entertaining boxers, so more people were buying tickets for that fight rather than the Tyson-Mathis bout.

"Truthfully, several boxing writers admitted to me that they were only interested in the grudge match between Terry and me. I honestly believe that feigning an injury for Tyson was easier than conceding that another promoter had a more successful boxing venue on tap the same day."

When the fight was postponed, Paul could have bailed out of the contract. "But I didn't. Those who said I was scared didn't know what they were talking about. I had to fight Terry Norris. All I asked was, 'Where and when?'

"The rescheduling was the worst thing that could have happened to me because I'd have to start over and do an additional training camp."

Paul had another take on the cancellation. "My spiritual side feels that God taught me a lesson by humbling myself in a situation where I'd be least likely to be humbled. I'd taken it upon myself to teach Terry a lesson. I was still angry about the comments he'd made about my dad. I'd succumbed to Kelly's advances and given her what she wanted, not because I was into her, but because I chose to. I'd never thought of her at any moment of my life until Terry made that remark!

"I'd written a poem to Terry in *The Ring* magazine describing what I was going to do to Terry when we fought. I'd never done anything like that before in my entire boxing career. I was quoted by the magazine that 'I was the force sent here to teach Terry a lesson for being such an evil person.'"

The postponed fight would take place instead at the Philadelphia Spectrum on December 16.

The Spectrum was the home of the Philadelphia Flyers, the NHL professional team. It was also the home of the 76ers, the NBA team. With a seating capacity of 18,000, it was the right size for a special event of this magnitude.

For Paul, however, it didn't have the same excitement and appeal as Vegas. There was another problem.

After maintaining his standard pre-fight training and 30-day regimen of eating and drinking only once per day, Paul arrived in Philadelphia 29 pounds lighter but still 6 pounds over the junior middleweight limit of 154 lbs.

The pressure and strict training program—jogging, dieting, sitting in a sauna in a wet suit and trying to sweat off the pounds—was more challenging than Paul wanted to admit.

"I didn't care if Terry was mad at me or not. I welcomed the chance to fight him and felt I was going to knock him out. In fact, that was the only script I visualized—to prepare to knock out Terry. I always found a way to win. This would be no exception.

"Then I asked a question I'd never asked before. I asked Arnie, 'What if I lose? What happens?'"

The night of the fight arrived and Paul stepped into the ring, ready to face not just an opponent but also a person with whom he had personal issues. One could feel the electricity in the air as the fight began. But after 12 rounds of uneventful fighting the judges declared Terry Norris the winner by unanimous decision.

Predictably, the *San Diego Union Tribune* positioned Paul's loss as a front page news story. When he'd *won the title* a few months earlier, it was written up in the back section of the sports page!

Paul was determined to brush off the media's deliberate disrespect. He would come back stronger and show the public, especially the San Diego press that he was unbreakable. He would not succumb to the critics. He was too strong for that.

It was time to get on with his career. Wasn't this, after all, what "Answer the Bell" was all about?

"During the fight, when things weren't going my way, I could have bailed out. I didn't. I went the distance—the full 12 rounds. I understood the lesson. I got it. Everything I did during the Terry Norris dilemma was wrong. Once I understood that, I was thankful for the lesson. It was all about personal growth. Truthfully, the fight was a showcase that God had chosen for me to 'open my eyes and teach me.' That lesson was: 'I'm not worthy to judge Terry, only God is.'

"The other issue I had to deal with involved Lisa. Now that I'd finally lost, people started to blame *her*! Even Arnie, my manager, had a comment: 'Maybe Paul's having problems with Lisa.'

"These remarks really pissed me off. My response to Arnie was, 'When you lose, you lose with grace.' This woman had brought so much to my life. They had no idea what she'd done for me.

"A lot changed on the night of the fight. I remembered that Sugar Ray Leonard had lost his first professional fight to 'boxing legend' Roberto Duran. He lost with class. He didn't like Duran, but he lost gracefully. As for myself, I didn't enjoy losing to Terry, but I got the message.

"Even though my confidence had been shaken because I hadn't lost a fight since I was an amateur, I realize I'd started to question if God was going to continue the lesson/punishment because of my romance with Kelly.

"This questioning was having a negative effect on my performance. I had a talk with myself. I was still 'The Ultimate' and I knew it. *I would be back in the ring again.* I'm a good student, I told myself. I'd learn from this."

As the new year of 1996 was approaching, Paul decided he would make some valid changes. For starts, he decided to elevate his weight class. He realized this was an important step in order to secure future success in the ring.

The drastic regimen of losing so much weight to qualify for the Norris bout had taken a lot out of him. It was grueling and had tested him to the max.

Added to adjustments to his professional career were personal ones. Lisa and he had just found the right home and they were planning to move in on his birthday, December 29.

In February, 1996, Lisa was transferred from the Sunnyvale office to San Diego. No longer would Paul have to fly or drive to San Jose. Life would be easier. With Lisa there, he was ready to get back into the ring. A fight was already scheduled for May 18 at The Mirage in Las Vegas.

Once again, the routine of getting into shape for the upcoming May fight took over. "I couldn't make 154 lbs. without training crazy hard. My natural weight at that time was 178 lbs."

Paul's opponent for the May Las Vegas event would be Clem Tucker, Jr. A cocky, self-assured, undefeated fighter, he came to the ring very confident in light of Paul's loss to Terry.

"Clem boasted he would knock me out in three rounds! I believe this was a fight where Don King and his associates thought Clem Tucker, Jr. would be up against the same person who fought Terry Norris in Philly and this would catapult his career, finishing me off."

How wrong they were. Tucker was no match for the faster, quicker and stronger Paul Vaden. "The Ultimate" won in the 6th round, a TKO. Tucker also ended up with detached retinas in both eyes.

May 18, 1996 - Las Vegas, NV - After landing a left uppercut on Clem Tucker, Jr., before stopping him in the 6th round

More changes, in addition to his entry in a new weight class, were about to occur. Lisa had some news for Paul. She told him she was pregnant. Already engaged, they decided on a date and they were married on July 5, 1996.

A few months later, on October 5, 1996, Paul was the victor of a 10-round fight by unanimous decision against Bernice Barber. He was now ready for any and all eventualities that would come his way.

He wouldn't have to wait very long. Instead of challenges in the ring and other demands of his profession, this new event would require a different kind of attention that would be equally important. It would be another milestone for the champ—one he would welcome and fully embrace.

On Sunday, December 8, 1996, Lisa gave birth to a son at Mercy Hospital. "It had been a difficult pregnancy. Even though we had prepared for a natural birth, complications set in during labor and it was not to be. The baby's birth required an emergency c/section. Weighing in at 7 lbs., 8 ozs., Dayne Christopher Vaden came into the world at 5:30 PM.

"My dad died on a Sunday. Since that time, that particular day at the beginning of the week was connected to a feeling of sadness. The script for my life had just changed. My happiest day ever, fell on a Sunday!"

Scripps Mercy, the same hospital where Paul had been born and where his father had spent so many years as a member of the staff, was now the birthplace of his son.

When Paul saw his baby for the first time, he felt the pride, happiness and love of fatherhood and parenthood. The beaming father called his mom and told her of the birth of her grandson.

Then Paul took the elevator down to the hospital basement to his father's former office to perform another important ritual. He stood in front of the door and touched the handle, just as he had done in 1992 shortly after his father's death. "It was a symbolic gesture to let Dad know first-hand that he wasn't forgotten."

That gesture was yet another bonding that secured the Vaden legacy. Paul would raise his son to have the same values his parents had handed down to him. Little Dayne would learn about courage, determination and perseverance. Dayne Christopher Vaden would become a champ in life, just like his dad—and granddad.

15
Life Call: Weighing In

Paul had now added another dimension to his life. As a father, he was determined to be there for Lisa and Dayne.

On Dayne's first birthday in 1997, he made sure he was in town to celebrate the big occasion. It was a bittersweet moment for him. A few days earlier in Pompano Beach, Florida, he'd lost by a TKO in a hard fight against WBC middleweight champion Keith Holmes.

"Abel Sanchez was back in my camp. I'd won earlier that year against Wayne Powell in Shreveport, Louisiana. The Holmes fight lasted until the 11th round."

As he approached his thirtieth birthday, Paul's interest started to expand to include other pursuits that would keep him more grounded in San Diego so he could be present for important events in his young son's life: his first walk, his first audible sentence, and holiday times with his new family.

One of the areas that started to take off and get a great deal of notice was the new exercise regimen known as Tae-Bo. "I personally was never really interested in Tae-Bo. But given its popularity, I wanted to incorporate my knowledge in the ring with a program that would interest the general public. My program would be a scaled-down version of my boxing workouts.

"I remember reading the back cover of a VHS endorsement from one of the Tae-Bo clients. She stated that after learning Tae-Bo she would no longer be afraid to take a walk by herself or park her car in a lot where no one else might be around.

"I realized that although Tae-Bo is a sensational workout and helps build self-confidence, it does not provide the level of self-protection this woman was looking for. I decided I would offer both a challenging workout for toning the body as well as self-protection tools and techniques for situations such as the ones this woman had described."

What emerged was a unique approach that only a seasoned boxer like Paul Vaden could create. "In the early part of 1998 I started going to a kick-boxing gym." This kept him close to home and gave him a different discipline to explore.

"People would come up and say hello and tell me I was a great role model, that perhaps I should seriously consider sharing my expertise with others.

"I was still boxing, but I wanted to branch out. After speaking to a few individuals, I was given carte blanche by the owner to use the entire gym, if needed, to train prospective clients."

Paul combined his boxing expertise—Vaden-style footwork and lightning speed—with powerful self-defense techniques and called the program "The Ultimate Workout." He distributed flyers throughout the San Diego area, inviting potential clients to experience his program.

"I needed to be stimulated by something and I felt this was a good avenue to explore. It was more of a hobby to occupy my time and keep me focused."

The venture proved to be highly successful. "This new self-styled program was a way to move beyond boxing without totally divorcing myself from my sport. I wanted my program to provide both physical training and mental conditioning."

Soon people started calling, his connections grew and the program started to take off. Paul was getting prestigious clients from upscale San Diego suburbs, including Rancho Santa Fe, Del Mar and La Jolla. "I created such a buzz among my clients, I decided to customize my demonstrations and expand the program to include seminars."

Paul decided this new venture would be about personal growth, not only for his clients, but for himself as well. "I didn't want to go the traditional route. I rarely go that route in anything I do. I did start a high-skills level physical workout, but I wasn't out to make boxing champions. Instead, I wanted clients to come away feeling better about themselves, both physically and mentally."

This new dimension to Paul's career reflected the changes that had taken place in his life. Now a proud father, he wanted to spend more time with his growing toddler. He helped his wife with the chores, changed diapers and spent more time at home.

Yet, he was a boxer. It was in his blood. He also knew the boxing world was still waiting for him to return to the ring. This part of his life wasn't over yet.

In early 1999, Paul decided to start preparing for his boxing comeback. "I was now a free agent. It was time to consider prospective managers and promoters, so I met in Vegas with manager Stan Hoffman and on another occasion, with Mark Stewart, my former promoter before I signed with Don King.

"Also, I met with David Love, who was my trainer from 1994-1996 before we split. I was comfortable with David and felt it was best to go with him, so I rehired him."

The next line of duty was to get back into training, to return to top physical form. Predictably, he launched into a strict exercise and diet program and the results were astounding. His weight had gone up to 208 lbs. and his goal was to drop 54 of those pounds, to bring his weight down to 154. He hadn't fought in 18 months.

To achieve his weight loss goal would mean total dedication to his mission and putting everything else on hold. For others such challenges might be daunting, but for Paul Vaden, they were merely another way to "Answer the Bell" and get the job done.

"A fight scheduled with Edwin Rodriguez in April didn't pan out, but on June 19, 1999, my return would occur at New York's Madison Square Garden to fight title challenger Jorge Luis Vado in the junior middleweight division."

Paul won the fight, proving his speed and effective uppercuts were still intact. It was a TKO in the 6th round.

It felt good for him to return to the ring and to emerge triumphant once again. It was also good to be in New York. His roots were here—his dad had been born in Brooklyn and had lived there as a child. Paul also had relatives and loyal fans in the city.

Even though he enjoyed his visit to the East Coast, Paul was eager to return to his home in San Diego to spend time with his son, now nearly three.

Although 1999 had been a year with victories and other positive achievements, it had also included some painful events.

On January 3, 1999, Ryan Cheatham, a cousin and the son of Paul's Uncle Ron, committed suicide. Ryan had just turned 21 on December 30. The event was a shock to everyone; his father took it especially hard.

"Why would he want to end his life?" Paul asked himself. He had known Ryan since he was five years old and remembered him as a special kid full of fun. "He loved being around me. I can remember when we lived in Washington State, he had this unique ability to hide and try to scare me if I was taking a shower or just in my room reading.

"I was very shaken by his death. In fact, I was so affected by it, I wouldn't go into my room if Lisa wasn't there, thinking Ryan was going to play that game of trying to hide and scare me at the most opportune time.

"Ryan was the first family member to make it to Vegas the evening before my fight with Pettway. He got to sit in with me during the media interviews with the broadcasters the night before. He was also in my dressing room during the entire time before my title fight and got to do 'The Walk,' with me."

Paul's Uncle Ron was so broken he tried to take his own life. Miraculously he survived, but despite the warmth and caring of family and friends, his feelings of guilt and anger were so overwhelming, he couldn't seem to move past his grief. Paul flew to Washington State for the funeral and comforted his uncle as best as he could. When he returned, he called him three times a day.

The experience made Paul realize how precious life was. When he was in Washington for the funeral, he was eager to return to San Diego to be there for Dayne.

"I was very concerned for Uncle Ron. I asked him face to face, how could I be sure he wouldn't try to take his life again? He looked me in the eye and promised me he wouldn't. I guess the pain was far too intense for him to keep the promise."

Through the summer months of '99 when Paul was in strict training for another scheduled fight, he continued to stay in constant touch with his uncle. And then, on August 9, he received news that he'd been dreading.

"I was on the freeway and was going to call Uncle Ron, but for some reason, I waited until I reached the boxing gym parking lot.

"Uncle Ron had successfully taken his life, this time using a shotgun. I was so numb I couldn't feel my legs. Thank God I wasn't driving.

"Once again, I returned to Tacoma for another sad event." Training preparation had to be put on hold.

It was a difficult time for the family and equally hard on Paul. He had witnessed the loss of two important people in his life. Life's unexpected events whether by natural cause, such as a 7.0 earthquake or a major hurricane, were one thing; it was another thing to take it upon oneself to create that event.

As the summer ended and the fall season arrived, Paul was again asked to demonstrate his prowess in the ring. The event was booked for November 20, 1999 in Atlantic City, New Jersey, at Donald Trump's majestic Taj Mahal Hotel and Casino. It was a good venue full of promise: a title fight for the junior middleweight championship. It would be a 12-round fight that favored Paul.

This fight would turn out to be one unlike any other in which Paul had ever participated.

"There are moments in your life when challenges beat you down, and you have a minute to make a decision. 'Answering the Bell' is getting up in the face of life's challenges when that bell rings. 'Answer the Bell' is unrelenting. Once you relent you become like everyone else."

–Paul Vaden

16
Answering The Bell

Atlantic City's "Taj" was the largest hotel/resort/casino in the country before the Borgata eclipsed it in 2003. Large, bold and grandiose, the $1Billion structure was a showcase for the country's top celebrities and major sports events.

Atlantic City was always a big draw for the boxing world and the Taj was the perfect place to attract large crowds of fans on the East Coast eager to see a unique performance. The choice of the Taj for the Paul Vaden-Stephan Johnson title fight in the junior middleweight division would also give showman Donald Trump additional press.

Johnson, only five months younger than Paul, was a seasoned fighter from the Brooklyn projects, a product of Gleason's Gym. He had a total of 36 fights prior to the match in Atlantic City—more fights than Vaden. His record included matches with some of the best, including boxing legend Roy Jones, Jr., Vincent Pettway, and several other veterans. Johnson had won the last two fights before his match with Vaden. He was eager to fight the respected former title holder and was looking for an upset win.

For Paul Vaden, it would be a place to show he had traction and could still be a champ.

As the fight began, Johnson proved to be tenacious and as the rounds continued, some of the spectators thought Johnson had the upper hand. But by the end of the middle rounds a shift in momentum had occurred. The Vaden technique started to kick in, giving Paul the advantage. It was in the 10th round when events took a bad turn.

Vaden, true to form, executed a quick jab, Stephan wobbled backward, Vaden pursued him and grazed him with a right hand followed by a short left. The blows proved to be decisive. Johnson fell, his head bouncing off the bottom rope before hitting the canvas. Clearly he was in trouble. The fallen fighter was quickly attended to.

Although Johnson was still immobile and unresponsive, the triumphant Paul Vaden, like most of the spectators, was unaware of the gravity of the situation. It was another KO by Paul. He was greeted by cheers from the crowd.

Then Vaden, noticing the commotion, knew something was wrong. His aides reassured him that Johnson, although still motionless, would be okay.

"Someone in the ring told me they saw Stephan move his leg," Paul recalled, "but the movement was far from normal. Stephan left the ring on a stretcher. I was still in the ring. It was a very uncomfortable situation. I was ushered to the dressing room."

Once out of the dressing room Vaden was given a further assessment of his opponent. "It was there that I was told that Johnson was in trouble."

Stephan, unresponsive, was soon put on a ventilator. Doctors determined that the hits to his head were serious. "I felt bad—real bad for Stephan. I flew back to San Diego, totally preoccupied with the situation."

Over the next two weeks, Paul continued to check on Stephan's condition. His contact in New York was Bonnie Smith, Stephan Johnson's girlfriend.

As time went on, Stephan's condition worsened. Paul knew deep down that the outlook was dismal, yet he was grateful for Bonnie's candid assessment and her updates on Stephan's fight to survive.

"Bonnie called and gave me more news about Stephan." She told Paul that pneumonia had set in and the brain had swollen to the point where procedures to ease the swelling had been unsuccessful. He was comatose and not doing well.

Bonnie indicated that the condition, known as subdural hematoma, was life or death. The swelling was getting worse. She wanted to prepare Paul for what might ensue.

Paul appreciated Bonnie being there and helping him to cope with the situation. Tragedies sometimes have a way of bonding people who otherwise would have no contact. He was well aware of the pain she was also suffering.

"I had Stephan on my mind, yet I had to be a dad to my son and a husband to my wife. I remember taking Dayne to see the movie *Pokémon*. I tried to go on as usual and my family was very supportive. Everyone knew what I was going through."

On December 5, 1999, Paul's phone rang. It was an unidentified number but from area code 212, so he knew it was New York City. He hoped it wasn't the news he feared.

The call was from a family friend, Mercer Cook, representing the Johnson family. "I tried to be normal during this period. In fact, when Mercer Cook called I was watching my favorite football team, the Dallas Cowboys play the New England Patriots. I was in the kitchen and the kitchen phone was the closest. I picked it up and Mercer said simply, 'Stephan has gone home.'

"I remember thanking Mr. Cook and hanging up. I paused and looked at my wife. There was no need to say a word. I guess my face told it all. We hugged each other. Then I called my mom to tell her that Stephan had passed. It was the most difficult day of my life."

Despite the fact that Paul knew from Bonnie's continuous updates that Stephan's worsening condition showed little hope, the news that he was gone was like a bolt of lightning.

Fortunately, Paul had a strong support group, both locally and throughout the country. Team Vaden represented Paul at the memorial service in Stephan's Brooklyn church as well as at Gleason's Gym, the famous showplace where Johnson had sparred so many times and begun his career. Paul also issued a press statement.

"After that, I started having feelings in my head. I started having trouble sleeping. My son's birthday, just a few days after Stephan's death, was difficult for me. Dayne was going to be three years old. He needed me. I had to be strong for him, if for no one else. He needed to know I was there and wanted him to enjoy his birthday. But it was a very rough time."

Paul's friends continued to stay in touch, calling him frequently; friends and family reached out to let him know they understood what he was going through. Paul remained quiet, preferring to be alone.

The approaching Christmas holidays would be a blessing. Paul had made reservations for the three of them to spend Christmas with his in-laws in New Orleans. His wife, mom and friends encouraged him to keep the reservations, and they decided it would be the best way to lift their spirits. It would be a release for all of them.

Since Lisa's parents were divorced, they visited both parents but stayed with Lisa's mom, Evola Cornin. "We always stayed there, since Evola had the room and it gave Lisa a chance to bond with her mom."

Paul's cousin, Evi, who was Uncle Ron's daughter and Ryan's brother, also lived in New Orleans at the time. Evi's husband was an assistant football coach at Tulane University. She was also going through a tough time, still grieving over the loss of her father and brother. It was a bonding united in grief; the two were a source of comfort for each other.

"Evola Cornin, a native of New Orleans, is a great cook. She can put together a meal that could go on for hours! It was legendary New Orleans cooking. Plus, I loved being around her."

But Evola didn't have a monopoly on cuisine. Lisa's father, the late Howard Cornin, Sr., was also a great host and expert chef. Holiday cooking was good comfort food for Paul; the activity of preparing these special foods provided a good distraction. Both grandparents also had a wonderful time getting acquainted with little Dayne, their only grandchild.

Talking sports was another good diversion that offered Paul welcome solace. And then there was the city of New Orleans itself. An elixir for anyone with the blues, it was alive year round 24/7, and even more so during the holiday season.

The whole city was decked out with colored lights and decorations. There was so much to see and do! But Paul was not a tourist. He preferred to stay at home with his extended family. Let others walk the cobblestone streets of the French Quarter. Let others enjoy the all night gin joints, musical halls and Cajun cuisine... all of this was not for Paul at this time. Inside he remained very troubled.

On December 29, Paul celebrated his 32nd birthday with his family and in-laws. His father-in-law's cooking added much to ameliorate the internal conflict.

Paul was already thinking of his future. He knew that eventually he would have to make some decisions. Would he fight again? Was his heart still in it as before? What was the purpose of a win if it meant the death of one's opponent? Fighting to kill had never been Paul's objective. There was so much to sort out, so much to think about...

On New Year's Eve, the three flew back to San Diego.

"Shortly after we returned, we took Dayne to Legoland. When I was in the car alone, I let myself cry. I wouldn't let my son see me get this emotional.

"I was overwhelmed with the fear that I would die. It was a feeling that stayed with me and wouldn't go away. I prayed a lot, especially if my young son was in the car with me. I would plead to God, 'If anything bad is going to happen to me, please don't let it happen in front of my baby.' This was my routine prayer any time I was with Dayne. I really believed I was going to die and be paid back for what had transpired in the fight with Stephan.

"I think I was trying to counterpunch death itself, and be a step ahead just like I was in boxing. The stress started to affect my relationship with Lisa. I knew it was hard on her. I became more defensive and probably wasn't easy to live with. I knew I needed professional help. I was very upset with myself."

The blame and guilt that Paul Vaden felt is symptomatic of survivors, whether the death is caused by a car accident, plane crash or sports injury. Paul was convinced he was destined for something catastrophic.

"I visited a psychiatrist. He reinforced what I realized—that I would have to live with that night in Atlantic City, and I also had to get on with my life. I had a son and a wife, a loving mother, sister and brother, extended family and many friends and fans."

Yet the tension was there. It was most apparent with Lisa. His lack of sleep and struggle to come to terms with his fears were overpowering for her. "I was so obsessed with the thought of dying, I was scared to even jog! Panic attacks, fear and the thought of leaving my son fatherless went through my head daily.

Over the next few months as the new millennium began, Steve Farhood, a trusted and reputable writer who at the time of Stephan's accident was writing for *Boxing Monthly* but who'd formerly had a long career with *The Ring* magazine, contacted Paul.

"Steve had written the first *Ring* feature article about me, followed by many others. On the night of the Johnson fight he followed the ambulance to the hospital because he thought I'd be there and he wanted to support me. He's a true friend and the person I trust most in the boxing media."

Steve told Paul it was time for him to express himself to the boxing world. His fans were wondering if he would continue his boxing career.

"He was very reassuring and was the only person I would talk to because I knew he was the one person I could trust. In the interview I said: 'I had been looking for a sign. Is God telling me I shouldn't fight anymore? Of course, I feel responsible. I feel guilt. I was the last person to hit Stephan. The last person to be in the ring with him.'"

Paul expressed to Steve his innermost thoughts. "I told him I wasn't sleeping well and had a lot on my mind. Also that I had talked to my pastor and my family.

"I told Steve in the interview that my faith sustained me. I'm nothing without God. I just hope he forgives me—that's what was going on in my mind. I said I prayed a lot and that my pastor, like everyone else, told me to be positive and move on. I had a great upbringing from loving parents. I thought of my dad. Boxing was indeed my life. It had kept me off the streets and gave me a purpose.

"Boxing was my dream, my meal ticket. It had opened doors for me. It allowed me to travel to places where I would never have gone."

For Paul to completely divorce himself from his talent and his profession would be a major shift, one that would steer him into uncharted territory.

Opening up to Steve Farhood was cathartic for Paul, allowing him to rethink his return to the ring. Paul was glad to sit down with a person who was not only sympathetic but also a friend who wanted to help him get through this crisis.

"I knew I had to go on as a father and husband. I had obligations. Yet, there were tensions in my marriage. I tried to deal with them but it was difficult. I started training again."

Paul Vaden, the gold medalist in the 1989 Olympic Festival as well as the gold medalist in the U.S. Championships in 1990 and representative of his country in Moscow, the former junior-middle-weight world champion, had accomplished much. He'd set his goals high and like every achiever he had his share of challenges. But it was his tenacity, his determination to prove to himself and the rest of the world that he was a champ that defined him and gave him his identity.

At this point in his life, Paul knew he had to prove something else to himself: that he was still alive inside and that he had the will to live. He had to return to the ring. There was no way out. Boxing was his life and he would use it to get some much needed answers. He would not back down.

"I was upset with myself and needed to come back. Deep inside, I needed to know whether I was going to live or die. I had to find out where my life was headed."

That meant getting back into the ring to hear the final bell.

The training was difficult. Again Paul had to lose weight in order to compete for a scheduled bout. It would be another test for him, but he was already familiar with the routine. In true Vaden style, he set out to conquer himself and emerge a winner.

In April 2000 a 12-round fight was scheduled in Vegas against tough southpaw Jose Shibata Flores.

"I was training very hard. The training for my return to the ring was not therapeutic and would never be routine again. I strictly willed my way through it because I needed to know my fate.

"Even if the events in Atlantic City proved otherwise and Stephan had lived, I still would have retired from boxing. So, the upcoming fight was really all about me—I needed answers. I had to reach deep into my soul and answer the bell."

Paul had lost 38 lbs to make the junior middleweight limit for the fight. "The sparring was hard at first." Paul was afraid he was hurting his sparring partner. But with increased repetitions he became a little more comfortable as he got closer to the upcoming Vegas bout.

Others who had experienced the tragedy of an opponent's death—Emile Griffith and Ray "Boom-Boom" Mancini—had managed to get back into the ring. However, neither boxer was ever the same.

"Lisa was not at the fight. After attending a few fights, it became evident that it was too much for her nerves. Still obsessed over the fight with Johnson, I told Lisa by phone before departing for the arena that 'if anything happens to me tonight, you and Dayne are the most important people in my life.' I had to tell her that, because I'm not sure if Stephan got that chance to tell his fiancée. I'm not sure if my cousin Ryan or Uncle Ron got to do that, either."

The bout with Flores went on as scheduled. "The first four rounds, I was a shell of my former self—tentative, cautious and holding back. By the 5th round, I was hit by Flores and shaken up a bit. But I reacted and started to fight back. I was fighting to live. I wanted to live."

His old self returning, Paul regained his confidence. He was hit but he hit back. He endured and showed himself and everyone else that he could conquer his demons.

"When I heard the bell concluding the 12th and final round, I realized I was alive! And when they announced that Flores had won by a close decision, I was happy. From a career standpoint, I knew I wasn't emotionally invested in this fight. I had retired as a fighter in late 1999. Yet this was a victory of sorts. It was a victory for me because I came back to life again. Things started to clear up for me."

The events of Atlantic City couldn't be erased nor would he ever forget them. But Paul was now willing to reassess his career and get on with his life.

That April 2000 night in Vegas was another beginning for "The Ultimate." After the Vegas bout, Paul would answer the bell on his own terms.

He had the opportunity to meet Stephan Johnson's fiancée, Bonnie Smith, in person when invited to *The Early Show*, broadcast nationally on CBS. The interview, conducted by veteran former NBC *Today Show* host, Bryant Gumbel, was a chance for Paul and Bonnie to express their emotions and describe the trauma and subsequent bonding that had occurred after the fight in Atlantic City.

**August 7, 2001 – New York NY – Interview with Bryant Gumbel,
CBS *Early Show* host**

"I convinced Bonnie that the interview should be done as a tribute
to Stephan. Bryant Gumbel started by asking Bonnie why she and
Paul hadn't met. Bonnie answered that 'Paul lives in San Diego on
the other side of the country and I'm here in Brooklyn. We stayed in
touch and he called to get updates on Stephan's condition.'"

Gumbel asked her if she felt that Paul was responsible in any
way. Bonnie was graceful, stating, "Boxing is a rough sport and I
know Paul didn't want this to happen. He's suffering too. We kept
in touch and it meant a lot to me. Stephan was my fiancé and I miss
him. But no, Paul had no intention of having this happen."

Gumbel then asked Paul if he knew that Stephan had been
advised not to fight again after his bout earlier in 1999 in Ontario,
Canada. Paul told Gumbel: "No, I wasn't aware that his trainer had
told him not to fight."

Gumbel asked Bonnie if some changes should be made, such as
more regulations from the Boxing Commission when medical con-

cerns were at stake. On this note, she agreed that stricter guidelines should be implemented in order to avoid a future tragedy.

Gumbel then cited statistics regarding the number of boxers who had died from blows in the ring. The statistics reinforced the need for boxing authorities to consider changes. He ended the interview by thanking both Bonnie and Paul for sharing their feelings.

"Steve Farhood also came to the CBS Studios in New York to support me and do a boxing feature about me during my *Early Show* interview with Bryant Gumbel. What a loyal friend he is! Currently Steve is a boxing analyst for Showtime Television and writes for espn.com."

Paul had received other offers to appear on TV. "I had calls from the producers of *Nightline*, *Dateline* and other shows for interviews. My article was being published in the upcoming edition of *Men's Health*. But I made it clear to the media that I'd show up only if Bonnie were allowed to join me. I wanted her to get the opportunity to disclose her story, her hurt and pain, because she was being disrespected by many, including Stephan's mom and many others.

"Producer Andy Rothman of *The Early Show* agreed to my request. I was grateful, since I wasn't looking for opportunities. They were reaching out to me. I believe it was the right thing to do in giving Bonnie a chance. But, I had to talk her into it. She was nervous. It took a lot of courage for her to go through with the Gumbel interview."

Paul Vaden would not officially resign from boxing. Yet the April 2000 bout in Las Vegas would be his last professional fight. He had achieved his goal of being champion of the world and then had come back into the ring again after the Atlantic City tragedy to prove to himself that he was still very much alive.

Now he set out to answer his own bell by rededicating his life to others. He would incorporate the values he'd learned from his parents and a long list of mentors who had helped him mold his life.

The discipline, love of sport, respect for others and perseverance during the darkest times would translate into a solid motivational program. He would start by speaking to people of all ages, giving them an optimistic outlook and using his own life as an example.

September 25, 2008 - Las Vegas, NV- Following an "Answer the Bell" meeting with the late Terry Lanni, who at that time was Chairman of the Board and Chief Executive Officer of MGM Mirage Group, one of the world's leading hotel and gaming companies

The program that emerged would be vintage Paul Vaden—"The Ultimate" in his finest role. Part-instructor, part-entertainer, he would captivate his audiences in what would become his starring role. Using his own life as a catalyst for change, his mission would be not only to educate but also to leave people with an optimistic feeling that life's trials can be faced head-on and ultimately overcome.

In his "Answer the Bell" seminars, Paul would touch the hearts and minds of thousands of people.

17

Paul Vaden Redux

History often reminds us of heroes and charismatic figures who have managed to reenter the world to make an even greater contribution after their careers were deemed over. Paul Vaden is one of those individuals.

In the darkest hours, the values of faith, fair play and honesty sustained him. They would now serve him well, allowing him to reach out to others and enrich their lives by helping them realize their full potential.

Paul decided to build upon the unique skills developed and refined during his boxing career to create a motivational program that would attract people of all ages. His "Answer the Bell" package would include physical and mental fitness, and well-being. Part-salesman, part-teacher and mentor, Paul's message would be positive, compassionate and upbeat. It would also be practical and realistic. As soon as he launched his new program, he started to receive requests for speaking engagements.

People like his presentations because they feel as if he's speaking to each of them—and since he's been through it all himself, he understands about obstacles, distractions and setbacks.

One of Paul's most endearing qualities is the fact that he isn't afraid to share the highs and lows of his career. He tells people everything they want to know. Most important of all, his track record of having achieved his goals and fulfilling his dream of becoming a world champion boxer supports the advice he offers.

One of the many individuals enriched by Paul's program is Cary Mack of Southwest Value Partners. Southwest is one of San Diego's largest real estate investment firms, representing commercial and multifamily apartment units to hotels and commercial office towers. Mack is a managing partner. When asked about the impact Paul has made on his life, Mack is quick to respond: "I've known Paul for many years, having had the good fortune to train with him personally alongside both of my sons.

"Paul brings an uncommon credibility to the people he encounters, as a former world champion boxer and current professional. I believe him to be one of the most effective health and wellness mentors in the country."

Mack points out that Paul is "honorable, competent, focused and always a pleasure to work with. He has a devoted interest in all things excellent and brings a contagious enthusiasm for his life values to those around him."

Cary Mack's endorsement is duplicated by Gavin Daly, program director of Outdoor Outreach in downtown San Diego. Outdoor Outreach is a non-profit organization for at-risk and underprivileged youth. By providing outdoor activities to poor youths, it demonstrates positive human qualities of bonding, teamwork and shared responsibility. This is a unique opportunity for many inner-city kids to kayak, mountain climb, bicycle, surf and practice yoga. The programs provided by Outdoor Outreach are impressive as well as impacting.

Says Daly: "Paul speaks to our youth about his being surrounded by the negative cycles of gangs, poverty and violence while growing up in Southeast San Diego. He expresses that, by taking advantage of opportunities and with hard work and determination, he was able to make a better life for himself and eventually become a world champion. The message is helpful for our youth. It can lift them from the negativity that currently surrounds them. This is a powerful message—immensely powerful!"

Daly points out that "they can relate to Paul and leave the sessions feeling much better about themselves and their potential. Most important of all, they leave knowing they are capable of improving their quality of life through their own positive actions. Mr. Vaden is a welcome addition."

Paul's delivery is simple, direct, powerful and sincere. He comes to the podium totally unscripted. No Power Point or notes; it's all Paul.

In addition to speaking to groups, Paul also started to host free boxing clinics for needy youngsters in the San Diego area. He became a regular at the Big Brothers-Big Sisters of San Diego where he launched a free "Answer the Bell" boxing clinic.

Paul uses his own life as an example of how one person, through determination and a dream, can achieve success. To his young audience, Paul is a role model, the "real deal." This is his most important selling point.

Paul's emphasis on the values of hard work, persistence, setting a goal that is attainable and sticking to that goal, is at the core of the "Answer the Bell" program. States Paul E. Palmer, San Diego Chapter President and CEO of Big Brothers-Big Sisters: "Paul gives inspiration to the little brothers and sisters with a lesson that goals are achievable."

Following are excerpts from participants' feedback:

"Paul was very kind and generous with his attention to everyone."
—Jack

"Please pass along a big thanks to Paul for his time and dedication. Kids have to see a real hero that had problems and tribulations in their lives and stayed through to their goal and dreams."—Lupe

"It was awesome! Rosa and I had never done anything like that before and she told me how cool it was and how nice Paul was to all of us."—Valerie

"Tell Paul his time and advice is greatly appreciated. Got me seriously considering taking some classes (boxing)."—Jareth

Perhaps the most poignant comment was from Steven: "Paul did a great job taking the kids aside and giving them some much needed one-on-one attention. I cannot thank him enough and I think it's a great way to introduce the sport to these youngsters so they see boxing is not just fighting but a game of life."

**November 19, 2011 - Third Annual "Answer the Bell"
Boxing Adventure with San Diego Chapter/Big Brothers Big Sisters**

Howard Wright, Chairman of the Board of Pro-Kids Golf Academy, a local San Diego charity founded by his late father, Ernie Wright, Sr., who was Paul's first boxing manager, serves well over 2,200 multi-ethnic children in inner city San Diego. Wright has known Paul for over three decades and has followed his career in the ring. He is a loyal friend whose interest mirrors Paul's when helping at-risk youths. Howard's program attracts youngsters to the outdoors, introducing them to the green and teaching them a relatively unfamiliar sport.

When asked to comment on "Answer the Bell," Wright was eager to share his feelings: "Always in a humble fashion that ingratiates him to our children, Paul has routinely visited our facility while conveying where hard work and good ethics can lead you. Paul has always shown a strong interest in bettering the lives of people on all levels."

Calling him a champion in the ring and in life, Wright adds: "The kids are always delighted to see him whenever he visits."

In 2010 Paul visited San Diego's Mission Bay High School and spoke to the student body. With a population of 1,700 students, Mission Bay High's demographics reflect those of the city itself: 22% Hispanic, 22% Caucasian, 14% African American, 10% Asian, and 1% Native American. The multi-ethnic mix offers a perfect opportunity for addressing the concerns, fears and expectations of the next generation.

In a follow-up class exercise after Paul's speech, students were asked to evaluate his presentation. The response was overwhelming. Following are some of the comments:

Chris Boyd: "The presentation was good because he made goals and achieved them and he is from the same place I'm from. He never gave up, even when he went through something that most people would have just gave [sic] up."

Bertin Rodriguez: "'Answer the Bell' means to me that good sportsmanship is the thing to have. Not only on the field but also off. I really liked Paul Vaden because he showed you can be tough and be a kind person. I myself can relate to him a little. He taught me to be kinder and still be assertive. Also, train and practice for what you want and if you want it bad enough—you can achieve it."

Anthony Torrescano: "The presentation yesterday I did like because he (Vaden) had a goal since he was little and he strived to get what he always wanted to be and that was to be a world boxing champion. 'Answer the Bell' to me means that if you have a goal you have to sacrifice and work hard to meet that goal no matter what."

Anonymous: "I liked his presentation. I thought it was beneficial for all students and student-athletes. 'Answer the Bell' meant to not hold back, and to go after your dreams by being positive. I believe I am making good decisions in my life."

Ernesto Zavala: "I liked it because he expresses his feelings and experiences through his own career. This means that you should always try your hardest. Don't let anyone stop you from reaching your goal. Yes, because you should always try your hardest in everything you do no matter what happens."

Paul maintains a strong positive relationship with the school system that was responsible for his own education. During the time his young son Dayne was enrolled at the Bonita Country Day School from 2001-2005, he attended parent-teacher conferences and also volunteered his time for field trips. He chaperoned students to events and took an active role in the school's many activities.

"Paul was willing to meet with other parents through the planning stages of events and helped raise the school's income," says Principal Suzanne Catanzaro. "I am also most grateful to Mr. Vaden for his support of our physical education curriculum. He saw a need and filled it. He made a personal commitment to work with students. Twice a week, he would assume the role of PE teacher and work with the various grades at the school. He soon became the most favorite teacher!"

The "Answer the Bell" program includes educational and inspirational presentations and seminars for children of all ages as well as corporate executives and employees.

For Paul, the key components of success are discipline to a cause, respect for oneself and others, and the ability to adapt to different styles of life. These keys, he tells his audience, helped sustain him in good times and bad. His narrative is replete with references to his early years at the Jackie Robinson YMCA, where his dream of becoming a world champ began.

"I was eight years old the first time I boxed and I lost! I wanted a trophy. I was disappointed. Was I going to relent and give in? Or should I go back and try harder?"

Students are captivated and inspired, identifying with the story of his early years when he first discovered his dream:

"'Answer the Bell' started with me. Yes, I finally won my first trophy and learned to stay the course. Don't give up. Boxing became my Disneyland. By the time I was 13, I was the best in the nation in my age and weight category."

At this point, Paul gets a good laugh from the audience when he says, "I didn't even know you could eventually make money in boxing! I thought it was just for the fun and sport. This is how genuine my purpose was.

"I give back what was given to me. I'm my own person, just as you are. Don't be lured by anyone who tries to convince you to be someone else. Stay your own course.

"I wouldn't be here if I didn't 'Answer the Bell.' I wouldn't have had the chance to see the world if I didn't embrace my own uniqueness. People told me I shouldn't smile so much. Boxers don't do that. Oh really?!'"

Paul's vintage smile gives way to applause from the crowd. "I had to be me, I couldn't be a phony.

"We get good advice from our parents. My dad said, 'Be kind to everyone.' I never forgot that, even as I started to develop into an accomplished boxer. Boxing is an art form, and I made my style fit my program.

"Growing up, we didn't have a car, so I took the bus. Got to know the bus routes real good. Some of you know the routes—right?"

As the laughter subsides, Paul recalls his days at the Y, his emulation of both Muhammad Ali and Michael Jackson. "We need role models—people we'd like to be. They both served as an example of delivering the highest level of excellence.

"My steadfast, focused purpose was to be the best and to achieve a goal." He tells the students to always set the bar high. His humble upbringing serves as a perfect example for the young crowd. They are captivated by his rise to the top of the boxing world. He tells them about the difficulty of his diet and exercise regimen. "If you really want something in life, you don't give up. You don't say 'I can't.' You say: 'Why not me?'"

He tells the students to "treat people well, achieve the highest level in school and create your own film. You can be anything you want to be."

He points out the importance of school, family, positive values and strong role models. "We all need people who inspire us to go the distance. Don't be afraid to try. If your gut instinct says I think I can, DO IT!" Paul reminds the students that each of them is unique and should 'Answer the Bell.'"

October 27, 2012 - Surrounded by students as I sign autographs after giving a speech at Thurgood Marshall Middle School in San Diego, CA

At this point, Paul usually steps down from the podium and goes into the audience. The students stand up, shouting and clapping, giving him high fives.

Paul then proceeds to sign autographs, giving the students wrist bands with the words "Answer the Bell," answering questions and acknowledging their personal thanks.

Students and faculty alike feel inspired and enriched. They have just met a man who has renewed their confidence in themselves by demonstrating that despite all the hardships and roadblocks, everyone can be an achiever. Paul Vaden has become one of their heroes and role models.

18
The Hunger To Achieve

A person's journey in life takes many turns. Dreams and goals are not always attainable, yet the desire remains. Only the strong and tenacious persevere. For these rare individuals, nothing short of a catastrophe can interfere with their dream. A test of one's resolve is the ability to overcome obstacles, pitfalls and disappointments along the way.

Not everyone is up to the task. Meeting each challenge and coping with unexpected and often painful events in one's life is a testament to one's ability to "Answer the Bell." It is a test of one's resolve to keep on keeping on, even when the going is tough. Only a rare individual will be able to withstand the lure of a "quick fix" and the many other distractions that can easily take a person off course.

The curious, highly ambitious young man at the Jackie Robinson YMCA never had those problems. Paul Vaden had a dream and he never wavered. He set the bar high and boldly announced to everyone—family, friends, teachers, anyone who cared to listen—that one day he would be a world boxing champion.

Like his idols, Muhammad Ali and Michael Jackson, he was the rare individual tapped by fate for bigger and better things. That special dream was part of his DNA and no one could take it away from him. During his growing years, Paul never accepted excuses from himself and never asked for anything from anyone else.

Deep inside, the hunger to achieve was always present. He knew his goal and refused to yield to any temptation that could give him an easy way out, a faster route to success.

Whenever Paul experienced losses and was forced to confront tragedy, he suffered like any human, but he also accepted these experiences as part of his journey—and moved on. He never forgot the simple yet strong family values that set him up in life and gave him a solid foundation.

"In 2000, I read an Internet article about Terry Norris. It mentioned that Terry was being denied a Nevada boxing license because the commission felt he had early stages of 'pugilistic dementia' (punch-drunk syndrome). They went on to rightfully admonish his manager, Joe Sayatovich for even bringing him in to have his license reinstated, given his condition.

"I read this article following the fresh episode I had just endured with Stephan Johnson. I truly believe the New Jersey Athletic Commission slip-up put Nevada and other commissions on high alert in preventing another casualty. I was happy that Terry's request was denied. But I also felt bad for him. I can honestly say this would be the first time I'd experienced these feelings."

Paul knew he could be compassionate to his former opponent in the ring. "After what I encountered in 1999 with three deaths, I know too well that life is too short to hold onto the feelings about Terry that I'd stored inside."

July 14, 2001, Paul was driving to an amateur boxing show in San Diego. "As I arrived, I noticed Terry's sports car parked nearby. You have to understand that whenever Terry and I were in the same room, the tension was uncomfortable not only for us, but also for everyone around. I took a deep breath and got prepared for whatever would transpire.

"It had been six years since we'd fought, but we still disliked each other. However, as I stated, I had recently experienced new feelings.

"I extended my pleasantries with others as I made my way around the hall."

From the corner of his eye, Paul noticed someone approaching him. "I saw Terry walking in my direction. Not toward me, but passing my way. Normally we both would give each other chilling stares and such. But something forced my eyes to force his eyes back in my direction. When this happened, we gave each other a nod. I stopped him and said, 'What's up, man?'

"A reflex took over to hold out my hand, and he followed with a handshake!"

This encounter would be a turning point in the contentious relationship between the two champs. A simple nod followed by a handshake was all it took.

"From the moment this occurred, all the disdain and negativity for this man left my entire body."

November 11, 2010 - With Terry Norris at a professional fight card in San Diego, CA

For Paul, it was a cathartic moment that was part of his evolution in the post-boxing phase of his life. "Over the years we would run into each other at other events and the meetings were always cordial, with an embrace and quick talk. The last time I saw him was at a pro boxing show here in San Diego in November, 2010. We were both introduced into the ring and it was all love, all positive.

"I even ran into him with Dayne at Dave and Buster's Restaurant, and Terry was with his daughter. I snuck up on him from behind. I introduced Dayne to Mr. Norris as the 'first pro to defeat your dad, and one of the all-time greats!'

"I'm not saying by any imagination that we're the best of friends. But if you knew where we were, you'd understand how monumental this is. And it doesn't matter how he feels about me. It's how I now feel about him. I wish him nothing short of heaven. An ATB moment indeed! Something I saw honestly impossible became reality. We broke emotional bread."

Paul's life path had brought him full circle to his nemesis in the ring and in life. With his focus on his son and the need to heal and move on, the chance meeting with Terry Norris was another opportunity to grow by offering the one part of him that had been withheld until now. Letting the past die, he stepped forward with a proactive stance and broke down the wall of illusion. Terry Norris was human just like Paul Vaden and each had their own issues to overcome.

In his seminars, Paul continues to demonstrate this part of him that is willing go the extra mile, to forgive and make amends, with no animosity or regret. His message is simple and direct: "You can deal with your problems and heal—just as I did. Even during the down times, the worst possible circumstances, we can choose to submit to those fears lurking in the darkest recesses of our mind—or confront them head on."

Ultimately, "The Ultimate" learned that his greatest opponent was not the man in the ring who was ready to take him on, but the one inside who was asking him to test his strength of character.

The self-assured, cocky, quick-handed pugilist did not have to come to terms with himself, yet he chose to. Like the young kid years earlier at the Y, Paul proved he was determined and driven. He would also help others on their own journeys.

"Forget the accolades, the belts, trophies, fame and fortune," says Paul to his audience. "What's really important—what really matters—is knowing you can be there for others."

These achievements have given Paul his greatest satisfaction— and everyone who is touched by him is all the better for it.

"Answer the Bell" is not a one-man show of bravado and chest-thumping. Students, adults, corporate personnel and the sporting world view Paul Vaden as a "complete package": nothing pretentious, no phony displays. His audience feels the warmth, love and compassion of a person who is eager to help others feel the excitement of being and becoming the best they can be.

Onstage at the San Diego Juvenile Diabetes Research Foundation Annual Gala with Karen Creelman and the late Yvonne Polatchek

October 1, 2011 – Sharing a laugh after giving a speech at the International YMCA Convention

In 2010, Paul's message attracted the attention of Qualcomm, Inc., a mega-giant corporation headquartered in San Diego. Founded in 1985 by Irwin Jacobs, by 1992 it had extended its international reach to the ever-expanding market in cell phone, base stations and chips. Its success is worldwide with branches in Europe, Australia and Asia.

By 1997, Qualcomm had acquired Jack Murphy Stadium for a sum of $18 million, aptly renaming it Qualcomm Stadium. Located in Mission Valley, in 1998 it can boast of being the only stadium that hosted both the Super Bowl and the World Series in the same year.

Qualcomm became the perfect niche for Paul. Respected worldwide, they sought a competent, well-known individual with quick wit and an affable manner. Paul fit the bill. In 2010 he signed a contract with Qualcomm to serve as a mentor and team builder. This new role gave Paul the latitude to present to the corporate world his unique approach to positive thinking coupled with a sound fitness and exercise program.

When asked to assess Paul's character and capabilities, Qualcomm Vice Chairman Steve Altman stated: "I have known Paul Vaden for well over a decade. When you first meet Paul you realize he is a humble, modest and respectful man who is easy to talk with and who is as interested in learning about you, as you are in learning about him. As a former world champion and a person who therefore made his living beating up others in the ring, I have yet to come across a person who knows Paul who doesn't think as highly about him as I do.

"Paul has always faced the tremendous challenges in his life with optimism and confidence, knowing that his energy, focus and faith will allow him to overcome any such challenge or obstacle. He puts his family and friends before himself and is one of the most unselfish people I know. He strives every single day to better himself. He teaches others, and at the same time, asks questions and learns from others so that he can continually improve. He has generously contributed his time to helping out many charitable organizations. I consider myself very fortunate to have crossed paths with Paul Vaden and to be able to call him a friend."

Steve Altman's confidence in Paul was matched by solid results and also by innovations that became part of "Answer the Bell." Paul became Qualcomm's Global Health Promotion Advisor, giving seminars, attending meetings and participating in workplace decisions. Through his expertise, Paul has been able to oversee company health and wellness initiatives. This involved devising creative and groundbreaking programs that meet Qualcomm's standards.

In Paul's Qualcomm "Answer the Bell" seminars, employees learn about the virtues of good health with a managed diet and exercise regimen. His unique presentations are welcomed by corporate executives and personnel alike.

As an innovator, Paul coordinated and promoted company global flu shot campaigns and wireless "fitness health challenges" seminars that pitch the substance of his "Answer the Bell" program. He also stresses the importance of team building in the work environment.

The results have started to pay off. The Qualcomm workplace has become less stressful. Management and employees have realized the need to connect with each other in order to make the workplace more productive.

Paul's successful "Answer the Bell" program for Qualcomm demonstrates the importance of utilizing the abilities of experienced health and fitness individuals to help alleviate stress in the workplace.

Says Perry Falk, president of a large fleet of Ford, Lincoln and Infiniti car dealerships in nearby San Diego and Los Angeles: "Paul's success as a boxer is an inspiring story. He is of the highest character and a positive role model."

Paul's talents outside the ring have become legendary to companies, large and small. Recently he was asked by Dan Shea, owner of Donovan's Steak and Chop House with locations in San Diego and Phoenix, to give motivational strategy sessions to his employees.

Dan understands the value of Paul's message and Donovan's has benefited greatly from Paul's intervention.

Dan is proud to call Paul Vaden a good friend: "I have had the good fortune recently to retain Paul for periodic 'Answer the Bell' speaking events for Donovan's staff. After every speaking engagement, numerous employees convey to me how inspirational and well-spoken Paul is.

"Paul's extremely successful career, both as an amateur and professional boxer, has prepared him well to be in the limelight as an inspiring speaker. Paul would be a real asset to any organization that enlists his services. Having seen Paul in action first hand, I am confident of his abilities and what he brings to the table—a commitment to excellence!"

September 26, 2009 - Induction speech at the California Boxing Hall of Fame in Los Angeles, CA

126

Paul is also a mentor and strategic consultant to Kristin Farmer, CEO and Founder of ACES, (Autism Comprehensive Education Services). ACES addresses behavioral, social and educational needs of children with autism and Asperger's syndrome. Offering consulting services to families and school districts, its staff has benefited greatly by Paul's ATB motivational seminars.

"ACES is a supreme company that has been an enormous help to families of children with autism," says Paul. "Kristin is a remarkable soul fighting the good fight for others. I enjoy her immensely."

"When you look at videos and talk to people about Paul Vaden, what you see and hear is consistent with what I know today," says Kristin, "Paul Vaden is a leader for all, young and old. He is a role model and a mentor for children and adults. His values are rock solid and unwavering. He has such a special way of reaching out to today's youth and inspiring them. He knows how to encourage them and to help them find their internal motivation. He teaches children about respect for their mother and all others. He also has an anti-bullying campaign not only for teaching children but for all who are bullied.

"Paul has been an unrelenting positive force in my life, my children's lives and for ACES. Paul's mentoring of CEOs and C level staff is unparalleled. I have had several mentors in the past. They always focused on changing ACES to be like other corporate environments. Paul focuses on innovation, inspiration, motivation and pushes you to 'Answer the Bell' to stretch to that higher height.

"I will be forever grateful to Paul for his ability to problem solve through life's difficult challenges, no matter how tough the challenge. He is an unbelievable human being. He is a true winner in the ring and in life. Thank you, Paul, for teaching us all how to become a champion too."

States Charles Herring, President of WealthTV, a U.S.-based lifestyle and entertainment cable network: "Paul makes a great boxing commentator for WealthTV's live events. He's articulate, and charismatic. Most importantly, Paul has the professional expertise to boil down in simple terms exactly what's going on in the ring for the hardcore and casual fan alike.

November 3, 2012 - On the set of WealthTV Studios performing Boxing Analyst duties

"Paul not only lets our viewers know what a boxer needs to do to win in the ring, but he is also able to tell us how the boxer may be feeling.

"There are a lot of great life lessons to learn from the boxing game, and I'm pleased that Paul is opening up and sharing his wisdom with viewers."

From Attorney Jerry McMahon: "The best part about my training with Paul Vaden is that, when we sparred we followed this rule: I could hit him any time I could catch him, but he wasn't allowed to hit me.

"Paul's Answer the Bell transcends boxing and personal training. It embraces life's important lessons: Integrity; Commitment; and Honesty. It's far from fiction, it's about real life, captured in an entertaining way."

From David A. Corbin, CFA President & Chief Investment Officer, Corbin & Company, Fort Worth, TX: "Our firm is lucky to have Paul Vaden as part of our team. Some people talk to our company about 'playing like a champion.' Paul has taught our employees and me to BE champions. "Answer the Bell" gives you things that you need to not only be a winner in business, but in life as well. Whether it is speaking, mentoring, or coaching, Paul helps our people reach their potential."

Paul Vaden's "Answer the Bell" program has become extremely successful with growing companies as well. Among those is Underground Elephant, a leader in performance-based online marketing. Recently Underground Elephant was cited as the fastest growing private company in San Diego. A *PR Web* October 31, 2011 release pointed out that it had a growth rate that was more than triple than the second place recipient. The *San Diego Business Journal* cited Underground Elephant as "one of the top 10 places to work in San Diego."

Underground Elephant's innovative CEO and Founder, Jason Kulpa, has benefited greatly from Paul's ATB proactive approach with his employees. Says Kulpa: "Paul brings out the inner champion in all of us and personally taught me that, as a business owner, you cannot win every round. There are going to be days when everything seems to be going against you and you figuratively take a beating when it comes to the breaks.

"Paul, however, showed us that poise through rough parts was equally important as grace in the good. The economy has been difficult and there have been times where we just didn't want to come out of the corner for more economic pain. ATB was our battle cry and the driving force behind our success. Our hearts and minds were touched and guided by a true champion, both inside and outside the ring!"

The core of Paul's message, whether in a large auditorium at Patrick Henry High School or in a small room of corporate executives, is always the same: each person can make a difference if they choose to do so.

In 2012, Paul became a Jackie Robinson YMCA board member. "Things have come full circle for me. Here's where it all started, in my own neighborhood where people believed in me."

Paul now gives back to his local, regional and national communities with his message of hope over despair and triumph over adversity.

"Answer the Bell" inspires each of us to do and be our best. It gives us the strength to move on, even during those times when we feel we are challenged to the limit of our abilities. It is during those times that we can think of Paul and let his story give us the strength to keep moving forward.

Paul Vaden

Retired World Jr. Middleweight Boxing Champion
Motivational Speaker, Author, Corporate Mentor
& Consultant

Paul "The Ultimate" Vaden, born December 29, 1967 in San Diego, California, is a retired professional boxer and holder of the IBF light middleweight world championship from August 12, 1995 to December 16, 1995.

On August 12, 1995 at the MGM Grand Garden Arena in Las Vegas as a decided underdog, Vaden defeated Vincent Pettway by a 12th round TKO to win Pettway's IBF 154 lb title. Vaden compiled a professional record of 29–3 with 16 knockout victories, and one loss by knockout.

In 2000, Vaden created the "The Ultimate Workout," a high end residential workout. Vaden also consults as a fitness pro and has appeared on V-H1 & MTV Networks. Among his specialties are corporate development, corporate speaking, and TV boxing analysis.

Vaden is CEO/Founder of Answer the Bell, Inc., developed in 2009 as an extension of his mind-body corporate fitness and stress reduction programs.

www.answerthebell.com
www.paulvaden.com
www.youtube.com/PaulVaden

CPSIA information can be obtained at www.ICGtesting.com
Printed in the USA
LVOW022037300513

336265LV00016B/29/P